Minilessons for Math Practice

GRADES K-2

Rusty Bresser

Caren Holtzman

Math Solutions
Sausalito, CA

Math Solutions
150 Gate 5 Road
Sausalito, CA 94965
www.mathsolutions.com

Library of Congress Cataloging-in-Publication Data

Bresser, Rusty.
    Minilessons for math practice : grades K–2 / Rusty Bresser, Caren Holtzman.
          p. cm.
    Includes bibliographical references and index.
    ISBN-13: 978-0-941355-74-2
    ISBN-10: 0-941355-74-8
  1. Mathematics—Problems, exercises, etc.—Juvenile literature.
2. Mathematics—Study and teaching (Elementary)—Juvenile literature.
3. Problem solving—Study and teaching (Elementary)—Juvenile literature.
I. Holtzman, Caren. II. Title.
    QA43.B7295 2006
    372.7—dc22

                                                                2006017051

Editor: Toby Gordon
Production: Melissa L. Inglis
Cover design: Jan Streitburger
Interior design: Catherine Hawkes/Cat & Mouse
Composition: Interactive Composition Corporation

Printed in the United States of America on acid-free paper
10 09   ML   4 5

SFI
CERTIFIED
SOURCING

FIBER USED IN THIS PRODUCT LINE
MEETS THE SOURCING REQUIREMENTS
OF THE SFI PROGRAM
WWW.SFIPROGRAM.ORG

A Message from Math Solutions

We at Math Solutions believe that teaching math well calls for increasing our understanding of the math we teach, seeking deeper insights into how children learn mathematics, and refining our lessons to best promote students' learning.

Math Solutions shares classroom-tested lessons and teaching expertise from our faculty of professional development instructors as well as from other respected math educators. Our publications are part of the nationwide effort we've made since 1984 that now includes

- more than five hundred face-to-face professional development programs each year for teachers and administrators in districts across the country;
- annually publishing professional development books, now totaling more than seventy titles and spanning the teaching of all math topics in kindergarten through grade 8;
- four series of videos for teachers, plus a video for parents, that show math lessons taught in actual classrooms;
- on-site visits to schools to help refine teaching strategies and assess student learning; and
- free online support, including grade-level lessons, book reviews, inservice information, and district feedback, all in our *Math Solutions Online Newsletter*.

For information about all of the products and services we have available, please visit our website at *www.mathsolutions.com*. You can also contact us to discuss math professional development needs by calling (800) 868-9092 or by sending an email to *info@mathsolutions.com*.

We're always eager for your feedback and interested in learning about your particular needs. We look forward to hearing from you.

Math Solutions®

Contents

Acknowledgments

We thank the following people for making this book possible: Marilyn Burns, for her guidance and support; Toby Gordon and Maryann Wickett, for their editorial expertise; and Melissa L. Inglis, for her work on the book's production.

Our sincerest appreciation to the educators and administrators who opened their classrooms to us: from Florence Elementary School, San Diego, CA: Principal Mary Estill, Elisabeth Frausto, Robin Gordon, and Frannie McKenzie; from Freese Elementary School, San Diego, CA: Principal Midge Backensto, Charlotte Odum, and Shawn Yoshimoto; from Jackson Elementary School, San Diego, CA: Principal Rupi Boyd and Sharon Fargason; and from Washington Elementary School, San Diego, CA: Principal Gilbert Gutierrez and Kimberly Sharman.

Introduction: Redefining Practice

Teachers have always known that their students require opportunities to practice the things they have learned. Opportunities for practice are particularly important in mathematics. When children learn a new skill or concept in math without having had the time to put that new idea into practice, they tend to forget what they've learned. Traditionally, practice has been synonymous with drill. The teacher models or introduces a procedure or math fact and then gives students worksheets full of problems so that they can "practice" over and over. The objective of this form of practice has often been memorization rather than understanding.

The purpose of *Minilessons for Math Practice, Grades K–2* is to broaden the notion of what it means to provide students with practice in mathematics. Instead of focusing just on facts, procedures, and memorization, the goal of this book is to give students ongoing experiences that will help them practice math concepts, skills, and processes so that they may deepen their understanding of mathematics and apply what they've learned to new problem situations.

Another goal of the book involves broadening classroom opportunities to do mathematics. There is limited time in the school day dedicated solely to math. This book looks at ways to insert mathematics throughout the students' day. *Minilessons for Math Practice* offers ideas for quick activities that can be used in various contexts. In addition, a goal of this book is to broaden the mathematics curriculum. Most teachers are required to use a district-adopted curriculum and have little extra time for supplemental materials. The activities in this book can be used with any existing math program to help students meet local, state, and national math standards.

Features of This Book

There are several key features in *Minilessons for Math Practice*. One feature is that the activities in it take little or no preparation. They are easy to implement. And the activities take only five to fifteen minutes to teach. Throughout the day teachers find themselves transitioning their students from one activity to another, from one place to another, or from one subject to another. These transitional times require teachers to focus the attention of their students so they can move smoothly through shifts in the day. The activities in this book convert these transitional times into rich mathematical events.

Another important feature is that all of the activities can be repeated. For example, many of the games in the book can be played throughout the year to give students ongoing practice with counting, adding, and subtracting. The *Quick Surveys* activity can be repeated simply by changing the survey question so that students can continue to practice analyzing data as the year progresses. In *Comparing Polygons*, you need only to offer students different polygons to compare in order to give them continued experience with two-dimensional shapes, even after your unit on geometry is over.

The lessons in *Minilessons for Math Practice* focus on questioning and classroom discussion. While the activities in the book are engaging and fun, they become mathematically loaded when the teacher spotlights the key mathematical concepts and skills. This spotlight becomes a focal point for the students when the teacher asks challenging questions and helps students develop their own language to describe their thinking and discoveries.

Organization of the Activities

The twenty-seven activities in this book offer experiences in all of the content areas important to elementary mathematics: number, measurement, geometry, data analysis and probability, and algebra. As well, the lessons model how to develop several important math processes: problem solving, reasoning and proof, communication, connections, and representation.

The activities are organized alphabetically. See the content matrix following this introduction to identify activities that fit the content area of choice. Many of the activities address more than one content area. The content area of focus for each vignette is highlighted in the content matrix with an X.

The activities in the book each have seven components:

1. the content area(s)
2. a materials list
3. an overview of the activity and an explanation of the mathematics involved

4. step-by-step teaching directions
5. a list of key questions to ask students during the lesson
6. a brief vignette from the classroom that describes how we taught the activity
7. ideas for extending the activity throughout the year

Getting Started

The activities provided in this book have been field-tested in diverse classroom settings. They typically take fifteen minutes or less. However, when introducing the activities to your students, you might find you need more time. In some cases it makes sense to budget a thirty- to forty-five-minute time slot for the first presentation of an activity. Much of the decision will depend on your students' prior experience and your goals for the session. Once you've made the initial time investment, the activities should run smoothly in a five- to fifteen-minute time slot for the rest of the year.

The lessons in *Minilessons for Math Practice* are language rich, allowing students to develop, organize, and explain their thinking. However, the ability to communicate mathematical ideas is a skill that develops over time. Your initial discussions with your students might be briefer and less profound than you had anticipated. Don't be discouraged. Over time, with good questions and a safe environment, students will become more confident and more competent in discussing their mathematical thinking. This is especially true for English language learners.

The key questions listed before each vignette and the descriptions of classroom interactions within the vignette give examples of activity structures that maximize participation and develop mathematical thinking and language. Notice that we use different types of questions throughout the activities. Some questions focus students on specific solutions, while other questions focus students on multiple approaches, strategies, or techniques.

Since the activities in this book are primarily for whole-class settings, we gave special thought to meeting the needs of diverse learners. The activities need to be accessible to all students while also being rich enough to engage all students at deep mathematical levels. Throughout the book, the vignettes model ways to encourage participation by all students and ways to help students develop the language and communication skills necessary for math talk.

We encourage you to use the book flexibly and adapt the activities to best meet your instructional goals and your students' needs. You might use the activities to supplement your current unit of study in mathematics. Alternatively, you might use some activities in *Minilessons for Math Practice* to keep past math studies fresh in your students' minds. Another option is to use activities as previews or introductions to upcoming units of study.

We recognize that classroom teachers face more and more challenges each year as they struggle to help their students meet local, state, and national standards and perform well on standardized tests. We hope that the activities in this book will support you in these efforts and we encourage you to use the book in ways that best meet the needs of your students.

However you choose to use the book, we hope you find effective and fun ways to engage your students mathematically. We also hope this book helps open your students' minds to math throughout each day and throughout the school year.

Contents Chart

Activity	Number & Operations	Algebra	Geometry	Measurement	Data Analysis & Probability	Grade Levels
Addition and Subtraction Word Problems	X					K, 1, 2
Addition and Subtraction Word Problems Extended	X					1, 2
Breaking Numbers Apart	X					K, 1, 2
Building the 1–100 Chart	X					K, 1, 2
Coins	X			X		K, 1, 2
Comparing Polygons			X			K, 1, 2
Cubes in a Tube		X				K, 1, 2
Dots	X					K, 1, 2
Estimating	X					K, 1, 2
Finding Friendly Numbers	X					2
Fit the Facts	X					K, 1, 2
Greater Than, Less Than, Is Equal To	X	X				K, 1, 2
Grow and Shrink	X					K, 1, 2
Guess My Number	X					K, 1, 2
Heavier or Lighter?				X		K, 1, 2
How Long? How Tall?				X		K, 1, 2
In One Minute				X		K, 1, 2
Measuring Area				X		K, 1, 2
More or Less? Version 1	X					K, 1, 2
More or Less? Version 2	X					2
Number Strings	X					1, 2
People Sorting		X				K, 1, 2
Quick Surveys	X				X	K, 1, 2
Race to 20	X					K, 1, 2
Sampling Tiles	X				X	K, 1, 2
Ten-Frames	X					K, 1, 2
Ten-Frames Cleared	X				X	K, 1, 2

Addition and Subtraction Word Problems

For Grades K–2

Overview

One way for the operations of addition and subtraction to be meaningful to children is by their manipulating concrete objects and connecting their actions to symbols. Children also extend their understanding of addition and subtraction by solving different types of word problems—ones that they read and ones that are read to them. This activity provides children with both of these experiences.

Carpenter et al. (1994, 1999) have identified four categories of addition and subtraction problems based on the type of action or relationship in the problems: join, separate, part-part-whole, and compare. (See pages 6–8 for some examples and definitions of these problems.) Children benefit from being able to solve all types of problems. When they are given a variety of problem types to solve, students become more proficient at determining which operation is called for. They learn that there are multiple interpretations of an operation. And they become flexible and efficient in their approaches to solving problems.

Young children solve addition and subtraction problems using a variety of strategies. Typically, very young children directly model the actions or relationships in a problem using concrete materials or their fingers. For example, a student solving $8 + 7$ might count out eight cubes, then count out seven cubes, and then count all the cubes to get fifteen.

As children mature and their number sense develops, they begin to use more efficient counting strategies. For example, a student solving $8 + 7$ might say, "Eight," and use her fingers to count on seven more to get fifteen. Eventually, students move from direct modeling and counting strategies to using their knowledge of number relationships to solve problems: "I know that seven plus seven is fourteen, and one more is fifteen."

CONTENT AREA

Number and Operations

MATERIALS

- *Ten Flashing Fireflies*, by Philemon Sturges (1995)
- $8\frac{1}{2}$-by-11-inch construction paper, 1 piece per student
- zip-top bags each containing 15 interlocking cubes, such as Multilink, Snap, or Unifix cubes, 1 bag per student
- chart paper and sticky notes

TIME

ten to fifteen minutes (twenty minutes to introduce the activity on the first day)

Activity Directions

1. Read the book *Ten Flashing Fireflies* aloud to students (optional).
2. Using a piece of construction paper and interlocking cubes, model a story problem for students to solve. For example, place three cubes on the paper (the "jar") and three cubes off the paper and ask the following part-part-whole problem (see page 6 for a definition of this problem type):

   There are three fireflies inside the jar and three fireflies outside the jar. How many fireflies are there altogether?

3. Elicit solution strategies from volunteers and record the strategies on the board.
4. Distribute one piece of construction paper and fifteen cubes to each student. Using the cubes, have students solve another story problem.
5. Direct students to each create their own story problem using the cubes. Write the following prompt on the board to help students get started:

   How many fireflies inside the jar? How many fireflies outside the jar? How many altogether?

6. Encourage students to share and solve their story problems.

Key Question

- How did you solve the problem? Explain.

From the Classroom

Charlotte Odum's kindergartners were seated on the rug in a circle, listening attentively as I read the book *Ten Flashing Fireflies,* by Philemon Sturges. Using a piece of literature isn't necessary for this activity; a teacher can make up story problems for students to solve or the students can make up their own stories. But children's literature can provide meaningful and interesting contexts for story problems.

I chose *Ten Flashing Fireflies* to launch this activity because it involves making combinations of ten, a friendly number to work with. This beautifully illustrated book is about two children who catch ten fireflies, putting them in a jar one by one. As the children in the story put each new firefly in their jar, the number of insects inside the jar increases and the number outside decreases. For example, the story begins with ten fireflies outside the jar and zero inside, then one inside and nine outside, and so on until there are ten fireflies inside the jar and zero outside.

When I finished reading the story, I placed a piece of construction paper in front of me on the rug. I also placed a small zip-top bag filled with fifteen Snap Cubes next to the paper.

"I'm going to make a firefly story of my own and have you solve the problem," I told the students. I then placed three cubes on the paper and three cubes on the rug next to the paper.

"Each cube stands for a firefly," I explained. Pointing to one group of cubes and then the other, I told my story. "I see three fireflies inside the jar and three fireflies outside the jar. How many fireflies are there altogether? Think about how to solve this problem, then tell your neighbor what you think."

Charlotte's students were used to sharing their thinking with one another. Since the beginning of the school year, Charlotte had been pairing up her students so that each child had a partner to confer with while working on mathematical tasks. Every few weeks, she changed these partnerships so that students would gain experience with different learners.

As the children discussed their thinking with one another, I listened in, impressed by how seriously they took the task. Charlotte had explicitly modeled for her students how to engage in a partner talk: turn your body so that you face your partner, maintain good eye contact, take turns sharing your ideas, be serious, and stay on topic. Giving students time to discuss and listen to one another's strategies for solving problems can create a cross-pollination of ideas. This talk is crucial for developing computational strategies.

I gave the students about two minutes to think and share, then to regain their attention, I counted down aloud from five to zero. Once I had their attention, I addressed the students. "How did you solve the problem? Raise your hand if you want to tell us your answer and explain."

"It's six," Shireka said. "I know that three and three makes six."

I modeled Shireka's idea by writing this equation on the board:

$$3 + 3 = 6$$

Tyrone explained, "I said three, then I said four, five, and then six."

Again, I recorded the strategy on the board so that students could see:

3, 4, 5, 6

Tyrone seemed to hold the three as a group in his head and then count on from there.

Jose went next. "I counted."

"How did you count?" I asked, prompting Jose, who seemed shy and hesitant, to elaborate.

"One, two, three, four, five, six," he said. "I looked at the cubes and counted."

"That's what I did," Vanessa told the class. "But I used my fingers." She held up her fingers and counted from one to six.

On the board, I recorded Jose and Vanessa's strategy of counting from one, or counting all cubes:

1, 2, 3, 4, 5, 6

"Other ideas?" I asked.

"I counted by twos!" Tony exclaimed.

"Come up and show us!" I responded, sharing his enthusiasm.

Tony knelt down next to me and counted the cubes on the paper and on the rug by twos, touching pairs of cubes at a time. The class counted with him. When he finished, I recorded his idea on the board:

2, 4, 6

The students' strategies for solving the problem represented the typical range for kindergartners and first graders. Some students counted from one; others counted on from three. One student counted by twos, while others already knew the number fact (3 + 3 is 6). I knew that with ongoing practice, the students would improve their ability to solve different types of problems, using more efficient strategies over time.

After posing the firefly story for the class to solve, I distributed to each student his or her own zip-top bag with fifteen Snap Cubes inside and a piece of construction paper. I then posed another firefly story for them to solve using their cubes. Finally, I directed students to each create their own firefly story and share the story with their partner and then with the class. To help students get started, I wrote the following questions on the board:

1. How many fireflies inside the jar?
2. How many fireflies outside the jar?
3. How many altogether?

All of the students created stories that involved numbers they could work with. I overheard Jose describe his story to Anjanea. "I see one firefly inside the jar and I see one firefly outside the jar. I see two fireflies."

Anjanea's story involved larger numbers. "I see ten fireflies inside the jar and five outside," she began. "There are fifteen fireflies altogether."

Extending the Activity

The following day, Charlotte posed another part-part-whole firefly story for her class to solve. This time, however, she wrote the story problem on a piece of chart paper for the children to read and then solve, using cubes if needed. She wrote the numbers in the story on sticky notes so she could change the numbers on subsequent days.

> *I see ⟨3⟩ fireflies inside the jar.*
> *I see ⟨6⟩ fireflies outside the jar.*
> *How many fireflies are there altogether?*

Each day for the next week or so, Charlotte began the mathematics period with a firefly story, using different numbers but keeping the same story context. She also experimented with other problem types. For example, one day Charlotte posed a particular type of subtraction problem called a separate–result unknown problem (see pages 7 and 8 for a definition of separate problems):

> *There were 8 fireflies inside the jar.*
> *The children took 6 out of the jar.*
> *How many fireflies were left inside the jar?*

Charlotte's students solved this problem in a variety of ways. Most students counted out eight cubes, took six cubes away, and then counted the cubes that were left over to arrive at an answer of two fireflies. A few students used their fingers, first showing eight fingers and then taking away six fingers. One kindergartner said, "Eight," and then counted back six to get an answer of two, using his fingers to keep track of the count.

Over time, solving different types of word problems helped Charlotte's students develop a repertoire of computational strategies and become more proficient at solving a variety of problems. Following are examples of some other kinds of problems that could be presented to kindergartners, first graders, or second graders.

Part-Part-Whole Problems

In part-part-whole problems, there is no action. Instead, relationships between a particular whole and its two separate parts are established. The unknown quantity (or part to be found or solved) can be in different places, depending on the story problem. Following are some examples:

Unknown	Example	Number Sentence
Change Unknown	I see 3 fireflies inside the jar. I see __ fireflies outside the jar. There are 10 fireflies altogether. How many fireflies are outside the jar?	$3 + \_\_ = 10$
Start Unknown	I see __ fireflies inside the jar. I see 2 fireflies outside the jar. There are 6 fireflies altogether. How many fireflies are inside the jar?	$\_\_ + 2 = 6$

Compare Problems

Like part-part-whole problems, compare problems involve relationships between quantities, but compare problems involve some kind of comparison between two distinct, unconnected sets. Following is an example:

I see 5 fireflies inside the jar.
I see 8 fireflies outside the jar.
How many more fireflies are outside the jar than inside it?

Join Problems

Join problems involve actions that increase a quantity. The unknown quantity can be in different places, depending on the story problem. Following are some examples:

Unknown	Example	Number Sentence
Result Unknown	There were 6 fireflies inside the jar. Seven more flew inside. How many fireflies are inside the jar now?	$6 + 7 = \underline{}$
Change Unknown	There were 5 fireflies inside the jar. Some more flew into the jar. Now there are 10 inside the jar. How many fireflies flew into the jar?	$5 + \underline{} = 10$
Start Unknown	There were some fireflies inside the jar. The children put 5 more in the jar. Now there are 10 fireflies inside the jar. How many were in the jar to start with?	$\underline{} + 5 = 10$

Separate Problems

Separate problems are similar to join problems. There is an action taking place, but in this case the initial quantity is decreased rather than increased. Like join problems and part-part-whole problems, the unknown quantity can be in different places, depending on the story problem. Following are some examples:

Unknown	Example	Number Sentence
Result Unknown	There were 8 fireflies inside the jar. The children took 6 out of the jar. How many fireflies were left inside the jar?	$8 - 6 = \underline{}$
Change Unknown	There were 6 fireflies inside the jar. The children took some out of the jar. Now there are 3 fireflies inside the jar. How many fireflies did the children take out?	$6 - \underline{} = 3$
Start Unknown	There were some fireflies inside the jar. The children took 3 out of the jar. Now there are 3 fireflies inside the jar. How many fireflies were in the jar to start with?	$\underline{} - 3 = 3$

Addition and Subtraction Word Problems Extended

For Grades 1–2

CONTENT AREA

Number and Operations

MATERIALS

- Optional: interlocking cubes, such as Multilink, Snap, or Unifix cubes, 100 per pair of students

TIME

fifteen minutes

Overview

In this activity, students continue to practice solving addition and subtraction word problems (see Chapter 1), this time solving problems with larger numbers.

Traditionally, students are taught standard algorithms (procedures) for solving addition and subtraction problems involving larger numbers, and teachers often expect them to employ these methods exclusively. Starting in the ones place and carrying the ten, and borrowing from the tens place and regrouping the ones, are time-honored procedures in the United States. Students usually learn these methods in a rote fashion with little understanding.

The goal of this math activity is to help students develop computational fluency with addition and subtraction. Students who are computationally fluent understand arithmetic operations, the base ten number system, and number relationships. They can solve problems accurately, efficiently, and with flexibility. Rather than always using a standard method of computing, these students draw on a repertoire of strategies when solving problems, and their choice of strategies often depends on the type of problem they are solving and the numbers involved. For example, a student might solve $39 + 16$ by rounding 39 to 40, adding $40 + 16$ to get 56, and then subtracting 1 from 56 to compensate for initially rounding 39 to 40. The number 39 in this problem is close to 40, which is easier, or friendlier, to work with when adding.

The key to success in this activity is communication. In order for students to become flexible problem solvers, they must be aware that numerous strategies for finding an answer may exist. By facilitating discussions, representing students' thinking in writing on the board, and posing problems that encourage the use of alternative strategies, teachers can help students attain computational fluency.

Activity Directions

1. Write a word problem on the board.
2. Together with the class, read the problem aloud.
3. Give students time to think quietly and then share their solution strategies with a partner.
4. Elicit solution strategies from volunteers and record each strategy on the board.

Key Questions

- What strategy did you use to solve the problem?
- Who would like to share a different way to solve the problem?

From the Classroom

Shawn Yoshimoto had spent a lot of time during the first weeks of school giving her second graders opportunities to practice discussing and listening to one another's mathematical ideas. So when I wrote on the board the following word problem for them to think about, solve, and then share their solutions with a partner, conversations flowed easily.

> *Mrs. Yoshimoto had 12 candies.*
> *Her friend gave her 8 more.*
> *How many candies does she have now?*

This problem is an example of a join–result unknown problem because it involves an action (giving a friend candy) that increases a quantity (see pages 6–8 for definitions and examples of different problem types).

I asked the students to read the problem aloud with me. Then I directed them to solve the problem and then share their solution with their partner.

After giving students time to think and talk with a partner, I called on Demonte.

"The answer is twenty," he said. "I did eight plus two and that's ten."

"Where did you get the two?" I asked.

"From the twelve. There's a ten and a two in twelve. Then I did ten plus ten and that makes twenty."

While listening to Demonte, I wrote his name on the board and carefully represented his strategy like this:

$$8 + 2 = 10$$
$$10 + 10 = 20$$

Demonte

Osman went next. He said, "I counted on from the twelve."

"Tell us how you counted," I said, prompting him to elaborate further.

Osman counted by ones from twelve to twenty. As he counted aloud, I recorded his name and strategy on the board:

12, 13, 14, . . . 20

Osman

There were no other different strategies forthcoming from the students, so I summed up the methods used.

"Demonte's strategy was to make tens, and Osman's strategy was to count on from the larger number. I'm going to leave their strategies written on the board and pose a new but similar problem for you to solve."

I wrote the following story problem on the board. As with the first problem, I deliberately chose numbers that would prompt students to use strategies like Demonte's (making a ten by joining the eight and the two), because they are efficient and make use of base ten ideas.

Mrs. Yoshimoto had 13 candies.
Her friend gave her 17 candies.
How many candies does she have now?

This problem is another example of a join–result unknown problem.

After reading the problem with the students and giving them time to think quietly and then share strategies with a partner, I called on Andrew.

"I made a ten from the seven and the three. Then I added the other two tens to get thirty."

"Where did you get the other two tens?" I asked.

"From the thirteen and the seventeen," Andrew replied.

I then paraphrased Andrew's idea to help clarify his strategy for the other children and to make sense of his thinking for myself.

"So you combined the seven and the three to make a ten," I said, pointing to the numbers in the story problem. "And then you added this ten [pointing to the 1 in 13] and this ten [pointing to the 1 in 17] to make twenty and added twenty to ten to get thirty?"

Andrew nodded in agreement. I then recorded his idea on the board:

7 + 3 = 10
10 + 10 = 20
20 + 10 = 30

Andrew

"I did mine sort of like Andrew's," Maria said. "But I started with the tens first. I did ten plus ten is twenty. Then I did three plus seven makes ten. Last I added twenty plus ten equals thirty."

$$10 + 10 = 20$$
$$3 + 7 = 10$$
$$20 + 10 = 30$$

Maria

"I put the problem up and down in my head," Xitlalic explained.
"You mean you thought of the problem vertically?" I asked her, writing the problem on the board like this:

$$\begin{array}{r} 17 \\ +13 \\ \hline \end{array}$$

"Yeah. Then I added seven plus three and that equaled ten. Then I put the ten on top of the other tens and left the zero below the seven and the three, and I did ten plus ten plus ten and that made thirty, so the answer is thirty."

I finished representing Xitlalic's strategy:

$$\begin{array}{r} 1 \\ 17 \\ +13 \\ \hline 30 \end{array}$$

Xitlalic

As I recorded her idea, I thought about Xitlalic's explanation. She had used the standard algorithm, yet she described the numbers in a way that assured me that she understood the quantities that the numbers represented (e.g., "I put the ten on top of the other tens"). Often when children use the standard algorithm for addition, they refer to the ten they are carrying as a one. This can cause students to think about the numbers in a multidigit problem only in terms of single digits, thus inhibiting their understanding of place value.

Yesenia shared her idea next. "I started with seventeen and I did seventeen plus ten is twenty-seven. Then I did twenty-seven plus three is thirty."

$$17 + 10 = 27$$
$$27 + 3 = 30$$

Yesenia

As I listened to students share their computational methods for solving this problem, I noticed that more students used their knowledge of tens for this problem than for the previous one. My purpose in this activity is to pose problems that are gradually more and more difficult, using similar numbers to encourage students to use computational strategies that make use of base ten number concepts. This does not mean that my goal is for all students to use the same method, however.

Judging from the students' solution strategies for the problem 17 + 13, they used several ways to combine the quantities utilizing their knowledge of tens and ones. For example, Maria started with the tens place first, combining groups of tens, and then added the ones, and finally combined the partial sums (10 + 10 is 20; 7 + 3 is 10; 20 + 10 is 30). Yesenia started with one number and then added tens and ones incrementally (17 + 10 is 27; 27 + 3 is 30). My goal is for students to develop a variety of efficient computational strategies that they understand.

The Next Day

The following day, Shawn continued this activity by posing another problem that was similar to the two previous problems:

Mr. Bresser had 26 candies.
His friend gave him 24 more.
How many candies does he have now?

After students discussed their methods with a partner, Shawn called for their attention and elicited these strategies from her students:

$$24 = 20 + 4$$
$$26 + 20 = 46$$
$$4 + 46 = 50$$

Tony

$$20 + 20 = 40$$
$$6 + 4 = 10$$
$$40 + 10 = 50$$

Tiyuana

$$
\begin{array}{r}
1 \\
26 \\
+24 \\
\hline
50
\end{array}
$$

Kierra

$$10 + 10 + 10 + 10 + 6 + 4 = 50$$

Eric

Continuing the Activity

Shawn posed story problems to her students throughout the school year. Her knowledge of the possible solution strategies students might use informed her decision to offer problems that might suggest certain strategies.

Just as we used 17 + 13 and 26 + 24 to prompt students to make tens, Shawn posed the following problem in hopes that her students might begin to create friendly numbers to work with by using compensation (taking away a certain amount from one number and adding the same amount to another number):

Jose had 39 cents.
Janelle gave him 16 cents.
Now how much money does Jose have?

The numbers in this problem prompted Tony to round 39 to the more friendly 40, then combine 40 and 16 to get 56. Finally, he subtracted 1 from the 56 to compensate for adding 1 to the 39. His answer: 55.

It was the first time anyone in the class had used a compensating strategy. Had Tony not used this method, Shawn might have suggested it to her students as an efficient way to solve this particular problem.

Finding friendly numbers to work with is a powerful strategy. To help her students begin to understand and use friendly numbers to solve problems, Shawn implemented the activity *Finding Friendly Numbers* (see page 58).

Posing Subtraction Word Problems

Subtraction problems are typically more difficult for students to solve than those involving addition. However, given practice, experience, and opportunities for shared dialogue, students will begin to use their knowledge of base ten number concepts to solve subtraction situations.

To begin, I wrote the following word problem on the board:

Tomas had 31 cents.
He gave 15 cents to Juan.
How much money does Tomas have left?

This problem is an example of a separate–result unknown problem because there is an action taking place (giving money to someone else) that decreases a quantity, and the result, or amount remaining, is unknown (see pages 6–8 for definitions of problem types).

As usual, I gave students some time to think and partner share before students reported strategies to the class. Following are the solution methods described by students:

$30 - 15 = 15$
$15 + 1 = 16$

Tony

$31 - 10 = 21$
$21 - 5 = 16$

Demonte

$30 - 10 = 20$
$20 - 5 = 15$
$15 + 1 = 16$

Alexis

$31 - 5 = 26$
$26 - 10 = 16$

Osman

$31, 30, 29, 28, 27, \ldots 16$

Keisha

$$\begin{array}{r} {}^{2}\!{}_{1} \\ \cancel{3}\,1 \\ -15 \\ \hline 16 \end{array}$$

Kierra

$15 + 15 = 30$
$30 + 1 = 31$
so, $15 + 1 = 16$

Maricella

Providing Support for Students

If students are having a difficult time thinking of different strategies other than counting or the standard algorithm for addition or subtraction, I might adjust the numbers in the problem (e.g., make them smaller) or use the following prompts and suggestions to help students:

- Try starting in the tens place.
- Is there a friendly number near (one of the numbers in the problem) that you can start with?
- Can you use addition to solve the problem?
- Try starting with the largest number, then subtracting tens, and then subtracting ones. (For $31 - 15$: $31 - 10 = 21$; $21 - 5 = 16$.)
- Use cubes or base ten blocks to model the problem.

Extending the Activity

Pose a variety of problem types for students to solve (see pages 6–8 for definitions and examples of different types of problems).

Breaking Numbers Apart

For Grades K-2

Overview

This activity gives students an opportunity to create equivalent expressions and explore number composition and part-whole relationships. In addition, *Breaking Numbers Apart* helps students develop a web of knowledge about a number, use operations flexibly, and recognize relationships between operations. It also provides exploration of key math ideas such as the commutative property of addition and multiplication (e.g., $30 = 10 + 20 = 20 + 10$; $6 \times 5 = 5 \times 6$).

Students are given a number and asked to break it apart, or decompose it, in a variety of ways (e.g., 25 can be $10 + 10 + 5$, $20 + 5$, or $15 + 10$). Knowing that numbers can be decomposed and recombined can be useful to students when they operate on numbers. For example, if a student is solving $28 + 35$, she might see that the 5 in 35 can be expressed as $3 + 2$; therefore, she could take the 2 and combine it with the 8 in 28 to create a ten (30) before completing the computation.

Some teachers use the date on a monthly calendar as the number students will break apart. Others keep track of how many days children have been in school and use that number to decompose. It is also helpful for students to use concrete materials when breaking numbers apart. Using interlocking cubes or coins, for example, can help children see the quantities that numbers represent.

Activity Directions

1. On chart paper, a whiteboard, a chalkboard, or an overhead transparency, record the number of the day.
2. If you want to let students use interlocking cubes, distribute these materials.
3. Direct students to think of different ways to break apart the number of the day.
4. List the number sentences that students suggest.

CONTENT AREA

Number and Operations

MATERIALS

- interlocking cubes, such as Multilink, Snap, or Unifix cubes, up to 100 per pair of students
- chart paper

TIME

ten minutes

Key Question

- In what ways can you break apart the number __?

From a Kindergarten and First-Grade Classroom

In the beginning of the school year, Frannie MacKenzie has her kindergartners and first graders break apart numbers from five to ten using interlocking cubes. Frannie wants her students to have a solid understanding of smaller numbers before breaking apart larger numbers. She also spends a lot of time discussing with her students how to appropriately use materials. Effectively managing materials is key to the success of this and other activities involving manipulatives.

For this activity, Frannie's students sat in a circle on the rug. After reviewing the rules for using materials, I distributed interlocking cubes by carefully pouring them out on the rug near the students so that each child had access to them. Next, I wrote the number *10* at the top of a piece of chart paper and directed students to count out ten cubes and snap them together to make a train.

"Now I want you to break apart your train in one place, so that you have two trains," I told the class. I held up a train of ten cubes that I had made and showed the students a couple of different ways they could break it apart. After giving the students a few seconds to work, I called for their attention and asked them to describe their trains.

"I have two trains," Carlos began. "One train has four cubes and the other has six."

I quickly drew a sketch of Carlos's trains on the class chart and wrote the corresponding number sentence underneath.

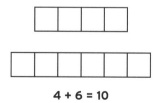

4 + 6 = 10

"Carlos has four cubes here," I said to the class, pointing to my sketch of the train with four cubes and to the number 4 in the number sentence. "And he has six cubes here." I pointed to the train with six cubes on the board and the 6 in the number sentence. "That makes ten cubes in all."

I continued to elicit the various ways that students had decomposed the number ten. Each time, I drew a sketch of the trains on the board with an accompanying number sentence. At one point in the lesson, the chart paper looked like this:

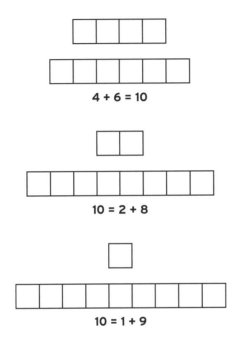

4 + 6 = 10

10 = 2 + 8

10 = 1 + 9

By the end of the activity, the chart was filled with the combinations that make ten using two addends. During the first few months of school, Frannie extended the activity to include ways to make each of the numbers from five to ten using more than two addends (e.g., $1 + 3 + 6 = 10$ and $2 + 3 + 1 + 4 = 10$). She displayed the class charts in the room for students to refer to.

From a Second-Grade Classroom

Like Frannie MacKenzie, Shawn Yoshimoto began the school year by having her second graders break apart small numbers from two to ten. As her students became more familiar with the activity, Shawn began to use the calendar to determine which number the students would work with. I visited the class on May 24, so I asked the students, "In what ways can you break apart the number twenty-four?"

Unlike the kindergartners and first graders in Frannie's class, these second graders did not have Snap Cubes to work with. All I needed for this activity was a piece of chart paper and a marker. The students were seated on the rug in the front of the room.

"Think about how you can break up the number twenty-four," I said to the students. I gave them about thirty seconds to think and share their thoughts with a partner.

"You could do ten plus ten plus four," Rosa said.

I recorded Rosa's idea on the board like this:

$$10 + 10 + 4 = 24$$

Lots of hands were in the air. Shawn's students were familiar with this activity and enjoyed it.

"How about ten times two plus four?" Tim said. Tim was one of those students who came to school with a strong sense of number and operations. He was one of the "experts" that we all learned from. I added his idea to the chart:

$$10 + 10 + 4 = 24$$
$$(10 \times 2) + 4 = 24$$

"Does anyone know why I put these parentheses around ten times two?" I asked, pointing to the equation and using my fingers to show what I meant by *parentheses*. The children looked puzzled.

"Writing a number sentence is sort of like writing a sentence using numbers rather than words," I explained. "If I use a comma in a sentence, it tells the reader to pause. If I put a period at the end of a sentence, what does it tell the reader to do?"

"Stop reading!" the students chorused.

"That's right," I said. "It's the same with a number sentence. I wrote parentheses around ten times two in Tim's number sentence because I want to tell the mathematician to multiply ten times two first and then add the four. Sometimes it matters which numbers you work with first."

"How about another way to break apart twenty-four?" I asked Danielle.

"Five plus five, plus five, plus five, plus four," she said. I wrote down her idea:

$$5 + 5 + 5 + 5 + 4 = 24$$

"Can we make a multiplication sentence using Danielle's idea?" I asked the class. Tim's hand quickly flew into the air, wiggling. My impulse used to be to call on students like Tim immediately. Now I wait and give others a chance to think and volunteer. If no one has an idea, I try to provide some help by asking a question.

"How many times did Danielle tell me to write the number five?" I asked.

"Four times," Toby replied. "Oh, I know! Five times four. It's like the number five, four times!"

I wrote this idea on the board:

5×4

"Is that enough?" I asked.

"You have to add the four," Danielle said, sounding confident and sure of herself.

"Like this?" I asked as I added her idea to the number sentence:

$5 \times 4 + 4 =$

"No! No!" several students protested.

"You need to put those marks around five times four," Keisha directed.

"You mean put parentheses around five times four?" I asked, fixing the equation.

$(5 \times 4) + 4 = 24$

"Other ways to break apart the number twenty-four?" I asked.

"Ten plus five, plus five, plus four," Shannon offered.

Now the chart paper looked like this:

$$10 + 10 + 4 = 24$$
$$(10 \times 2) + 4 = 24$$
$$5 + 5 + 5 + 5 + 4 = 24$$
$$(5 \times 4) + 4 = 24$$
$$10 + 5 + 5 + 4 = 24$$

"You could do one plus one plus one . . . all the way to twenty-four," Leo suggested.

"Yes, twenty-four is also made up of twenty-four ones," I confirmed as I wrote the long number sentence on the chart. When no one else had an idea, I suggested one myself. I often will do this to stretch students' thinking.

I wrote this equation on the chart:

$(5 \times 2) + (5 \times 2) + 4 = 24$

"What do you notice about my number sentence?" I asked the class.
"It's the same as Tim's!" Charlotte exclaimed.
"How's that?" I asked her.
"Well, five times two is the same thing as ten, and you do it two times, then add four," she explained.
"It has two . . . marks like you made," Jose said. "You multiply those first."
"It equals twenty-four," Toby observed. "They all do."

Extending the Activity

- Ask students to represent a number using coins.
- Use calculators.
- Introduce constraints:

    You must use only addition.
    You must use more than one operation.
    You must use at least three numbers.
    You can't use zero.

Building the 1–100 Chart

For Grades K-2

Overview

In this activity, students find the correct location of numbers in a 1–100 wall chart. The activity provides students with the opportunity to focus on an orderly arrangement of the numbers one through one hundred, identify and describe number patterns, and see the relationships between and among numbers. In *Building the 1–100 Chart*, students practice adding ten to a number and subtracting ten from a number. Being able to make leaps of ten helps children compute efficiently and signals an understanding of our base ten number system.

Activity Directions

1. For kindergartners and first graders, insert the number cards sequentially from 1 to 5 (as well as card 20) into the wall chart. For second graders, insert cards 1–15.
2. Explain to the children that you will show other number cards and ask for volunteers to figure out where they belong on the chart. Do not choose numbers sequentially.
3. As children place numbers on the chart, have them explain how they decided where to put them. If a child has difficulty explaining, have that child choose a volunteer to help.
4. Continue to have students place numbers on the chart over the next several days. Spreading the experience over a few class periods gives children time to reflect on the patterns that emerge in the chart.

Key Questions for Grades K-2

- What do you notice about the chart today?
- Where does this number fit in the chart? How do you know?

CONTENT AREA

Number and Operations

MATERIALS

- wall chart with a 10-by-10 array of transparent plastic pockets
- 100 cards to fit in the plastic pockets, numbered 1-100

TIME

five minutes (ten to fifteen minutes to introduce the activity on the first day)

Additional Key Questions for Grade 2

- What happens to a number when you add ten to it?
- What happens to a number when you subtract ten from it?

From a Kindergarten and First-Grade Classroom

To begin the activity, I showed Elisabeth Frausto's kindergartners and first graders the 1–100 chart that I had prepared. The chart was empty except for the numbers 1–5 and the number 20:

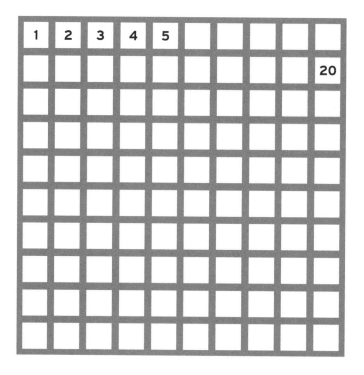

"What do you notice about the chart?" I asked the class. Elisabeth's students were familiar with the 1–100 chart. They had seen it before, complete with the numbers 1–100 filled in.

"Numbers are missing!" Donavyn exclaimed.

"The last number should be one hundred," Sophie said.

"You're correct," I acknowledged. "There are numbers missing from the chart. Today, I'm going to show you some of those missing numbers and see if you can figure out where they fit on the chart."

For second graders and sometimes for first graders, I have students build the entire 1–100 chart over time. For a K–1 classroom, I have students build only part of the 1–100 chart in order to give students lots of experience with a smaller range of numbers.

Holding the number cards 6–19 in my hand, I chose the card with the 6 to show the class first because it seemed like an easy place to start. After we read the number aloud together, I called on John. He quickly and confidently placed it next to the 5 on the chart.

"John, tell us how you know that six is in its correct place," I said.

"Six comes after five," he stated. "And five comes before six."

Knowing what number comes before a number and what number comes after a number is an important concept for primary students. This activity can help develop this key idea.

Next, I held up the number 15. I knew this might be a challenge for some students. After we read the number together, I called on Roger to come up and put the card in its correct place on the chart. Roger stared at the chart for a moment, hesitating. Then he put the number 15 where 17 should have gone.

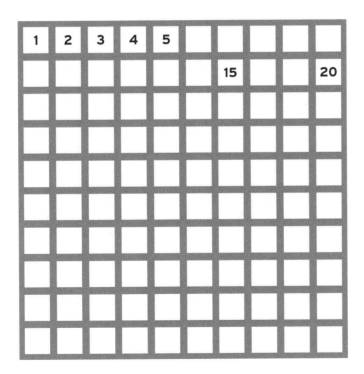

"How do you know that fifteen is in its correct place?" I asked.

"I'm not sure," Roger responded.

"How can you check?" I asked.

"Count!" Roger exclaimed. He then started counting on the chart from 1 to 20, pointing to each number or the empty space where each number should go. Roger soon figured out that he had made a mistake, but he didn't seem to know what to do about it.

"Do you want someone to help you?" I asked him. Roger then called on Angie to come up. She immediately took the 15 number card and placed it underneath the 5 on the number chart.

"How do you know that's correct?" I asked.

"'Cause it's a pattern," Angie said. "There's a five in fifteen and there's a five here," she said, pointing to the 5 in the numbers 5 and 15 on the chart.

Angie had noticed an important pattern. I wondered if other students would catch on. Next, I held up the number 13 and asked Jamal to come and put it in its correct place. He walked up and quickly fit it in the empty slot in the row directly underneath the number 3.

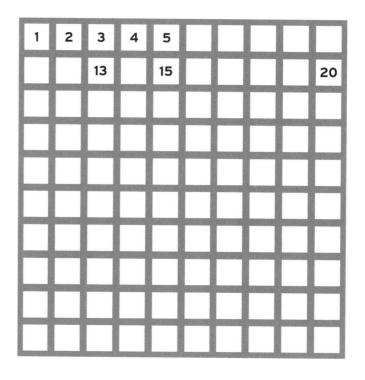

"How did you know so quickly?" I asked him.

"'Cause it's like Angie said," he began. "There's a three in thirteen, so I put it under the three."

"So where would the number twenty-three go?" I asked.

"Underneath the thirteen," he responded.

"And thirty-three—where would it go?" I probed.

By now, other students were catching on, and several called out in unison, "Under the twenty-three!"

I finished the activity by having one more student place a number card on the chart and explain why it fit there. For the next few days, Elisabeth started math class with this activity until all the numbers from 1 to 20 were filled in on the chart.

From a Second-Grade Classroom

Robin Gordon's second graders were settled on the rug, facing the 1–100 chart. Just before the lesson, I had removed all of the number cards in the chart except for the numbers 1–15.

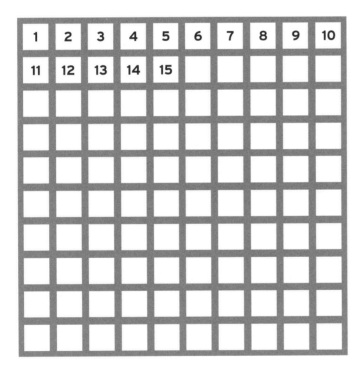

The children had worked with the chart the previous week and were accustomed to it being completely filled in with the numbers 1–100.

"What do you notice about the chart today?" I asked the class. "What's different about it?" I gave the students some think time before eliciting ideas.

"It's missing numbers," Tamika said.

Jose added, "There's only fifteen numbers on the chart today. Last week there were a hundred."

I had shuffled the remaining number cards and was holding the deck in my hand. I found the card that read 100 and showed it to the class, directing them to read it in a whisper voice.

"Think for a few seconds about where this card goes in the chart," I said. After a few seconds, I called on Sol, and he walked over to me, took the card, and placed it in the transparent pocket at the bottom right-hand corner of the chart.

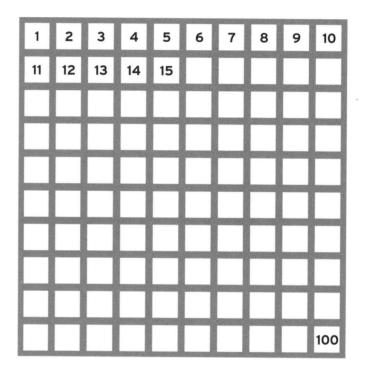

"Tell us how you knew to place the one-hundred card there," I said.

"Well, the chart goes to one hundred and this is the last place," he explained. "Anyway, I remembered the numbers from last week."

Next, I drew the number 54 from the deck and asked the class to read it aloud. I then directed the students to take a moment and think about where on the chart 54 would go. After a few seconds, I called on Jessica to place the number card in the pocket where she thought it belonged in the chart. Without hesitation, she slipped the card in the correct spot.

"I know it goes here because I looked at fourteen," she explained, pointing to the second row of numbers on the chart, "because there's a four in the ones, and then I counted by tens: fourteen, twenty-four, thirty-four, forty-four, and fifty-four."

"What happens to a number when you add ten to it?" I asked the class. "For example, Jessica started with fourteen and added ten to get to twenty-four, then added another ten to get thirty-four, another ten to get forty-four, and finally another ten to get fifty-four." I wrote the numbers on the board like this:

14

24

34

44

54

"What do you notice about the numbers when you add ten?" I asked.

"The numbers in the ones place stay the same; they all are four," Tomas observed.

"And the numbers in the tens place go up by one each time," Kate said.

"What if you subtract ten from a number?" I asked. I pointed to the 54 and slid my index finger up to the 44. "What happens to the digits in the ones place and the tens place when you subtract ten?"

"It's kind of opposite," River said. "The tens number goes down one and the one's place stays the same again."

Identifying and describing patterns in our number system is important. In this case, noticing what happens to the digits in a number when ten is added or subtracted can help students compute efficiently and accurately. Initially, we want students to spend time thinking about patterns and how they work, and later, we want them to apply their understanding to compute efficiently and accurately.

Next, I drew the number 23. After we read the number aloud, I called on River. He pointed to 15 on the chart and counted by ones to 23 and then placed the card in the chart. Then he faced the class and said, "I counted on from fifteen till I got to twenty-three."

Julia went next. At first, she had some difficulty deciding where to place the number 67, initially putting it where the number 65 should have gone.

She explained, "I know that the sixties go in this row 'cause Jessica put the fifty-four in the row above."

Julia pointed to the number 54 and said, "If fifty-four goes here, then I go down to sixty-four and go over to sixty-seven." Although Julia had made a mistake in placing the number card, I was impressed with the vocabulary she used to describe the movements on the chart: *row*, *above*, *over*, and *down*. In addition to helping students become familiar with our number system, placing numbers on the 1–100 chart also gives students practice with communicating their mathematical thinking.

"Count again to make sure," I suggested. Julia counted on from 64 and realized her mistake. She quickly corrected herself.

We completed the activity after five students had placed number cards in the 1–100 chart. Robin planned to continue the activity over the next few weeks, having about five students each day place number cards in the chart.

Extending the Activity

- After a student has placed a number in the 1–100 chart, ask the class which number would be ten more or ten less than the number placed in the chart. For kindergartners, ask which number would be one more or one less than the number placed in the chart.
- Once the 1–100 chart is completely filled in, have students practice counting by twos, fives, and tens. Point to the numbers in the chart to support students as they skip-count.

Coins

For Grades K-2

5

Overview

In this activity, students work to connect the correct names and values to pennies, nickels, dimes, and quarters. This activity provides experience and practice necessary for children to internalize the names and values of coins.

Students also learn how to find the total value of a collection of coins that are all the same and a collection of coins that are different. A child's ability to count a collection of coins depends on his or her number sense and ability to compute and recognize the value of the coins involved. Instead of telling children how to combine the quantities represented by the coins, you should encourage them to find the total amounts in ways that make sense to them. Through shared dialogue, students can learn about a variety of strategies to efficiently and accurately find the total value of a collection of coins. For example, if a student is asked to figure the total value of a quarter, two nickels, and a dime, there are several ways to solve the problem. She might start with 25, add 10 to make 35, add 5 to get to 40, and then finish by adding the last nickel to get a total of 45 cents. Or she could start with 25, add the two nickels to the dime to get 20, and then add 25 and 20 to make 45. She could also start with the nickel, add the second nickel to make 10 cents, add the dime to get to 20, add 20 from the quarter to get to 40, and then add the remaining 5 cents from the quarter to get to 45.

Activity Directions for Grades K-1

1. Distribute to each student a zip-top bag containing twenty pennies, ten nickels, ten dimes, and two quarters.
2. Ask students to sort the coins and find out how many pennies, nickels, dimes, and quarters they have.
3. Ask students how many coins they would have if you gave them one more and one less.
4. Hold up a coin so that everyone can see. Ask students the value of the coin. Repeat this procedure for different coins.

CONTENT AREA

Measurement

Number and Operations

MATERIALS

- zip-top bags with a collection of 20 pennies, 10 nickels, 10 dimes, and 2 quarters, 1 per student

TIME

ten minutes

5. Ask students to show a coin that is worth five cents, one that's worth ten cents, one that's worth the most amount of money, and one that's worth the least amount of money.
6. Work with the students who are ready for a challenge in small groups. Direct these students to place in front of them a collection of coins (e.g., a dime, a nickel, and a penny).
7. Ask each students to find the total value of the collection of coins, and elicit strategies for determining that value from the students.

Activity Directions for Grade 2

1. Distribute to each student a zip-top bag containing twenty pennies, ten nickels, ten dimes, and two quarters.
2. Ask students to sort the coins and identify the names and values of the coins.
3. Direct students to place in front of them a collection of coins (e.g., three dimes, three nickels, and sixteen pennies).
4. Ask each student to find the total value of the collection of coins, and elicit strategies for determining the value from the students.

Key Questions

- How many pennies do you have?
- If I gave you one more penny, then how many pennies would you have?
- If I took one penny away from you, how many would you have then?
- How many nickels, dimes, and quarters do you have?
- Who can show me a coin that is worth five cents?
- Who can show me a coin that is worth ten cents?
- Who can show me a coin that is worth the most amount of money?
- Who can show me a coin that is worth the least amount of money?
- How much is this collection of coins worth? Explain your thinking.
- Who solved it in a different way?

From a Kindergarten and First-Grade Classroom

Day 1

I quickly handed out a zip-top bag filled with coins to each student in Frannie MacKenzie's kindergarten and first-grade class. In each bag were twenty pennies, ten nickels, ten dimes, and two quarters.

"Sort your coins so that all of the pennies are together in a group, all the nickels are together, the dimes are together, and all the quarters are together," I directed.

We had been sorting and counting coins for several days and most of the students had learned the names and values. I circulated as students grouped their coins, observing who needed help sorting and quizzing a few students who I knew were still struggling with the coin names and values. A few children used the commercial poster that was hanging on the whiteboard to help them. The poster had pictures of all of the U.S. coins, their names, and their values. Once everyone had finished sorting, I asked a series of questions.

"Point to your pennies," I directed. "How many pennies do you have?"

Students began to count. When they were finished, I asked, "What if I gave you one more penny? Then how many pennies would you have? What if I took one penny away from you? How many would you have then?"

These questions seemed easy for most students. But I knew that some children, especially the kindergartners, were still learning the concepts of one more and one less. This was a good opportunity to give students practice with this important concept.

Next, I asked the students to count and find out how many nickels they had, then dimes, then quarters. I finished the activity by holding up different coins and asking how much each was worth. I then varied this activity by asking the following questions:

Who can show me a coin that is worth five cents?
Who can show me a coin that is worth ten cents?
Who can show me a coin that is worth the most amount of money?
Who can show me a coin that is worth the least amount of money?

This ended the whole-group portion of the *Coins* activity.

Day 2: Working with Small Groups

Because there is such a wide range of abilities in a K–1 classroom, especially when it comes to working with money, I decided to continue sorting and counting coins with students in small groups. Some of the kindergartners needed extra practice with identifying the names and values of the coins. Other students were ready for something more challenging.

One group of four students was ready to find the total value of a collection of coins. I began by directing the students to empty their bags and sort their coins into groups. Then I asked them to find the value of each group. For example, students counted by fives to determine the total value of their nickels and by tens to figure out the value of their dimes.

Next, I asked the students to determine the total value of a mixed collection of coins. For example, I showed them a nickel and a penny and asked them how much the two coins together were worth. This can be tricky for young children. Despite the fact that the words *five cents* are found on a nickel, there is nothing about the coin that shows the quantity five. Nevertheless, using coins to compute can help students count on from the larger quantity. I noticed this when students were figuring the total value of a nickel and a penny—all started with five and added on one more.

I continued to ask the students to find the value of different mixed collections of coins. For example:

1 dime, 1 nickel, 1 penny
1 penny, 2 nickels
2 dimes, 1 nickel, 2 pennies
1 nickel, 1 quarter, 1 penny
3 nickels, 1 dime, 1 penny

From a Second-Grade Classroom

With Robin Gordon's second graders, I began by handing out identical zip-top bags of coins to each student, each bag containing the same coins, and directing them to sort the coins and identify their names and values. The students were seated on the rug in a circle.

Next, I asked the students to put the following collection of coins in front of them on the carpet and figure the total:

3 nickels, 3 dimes, 16 pennies

After giving students time to work, I asked for their attention and called on Chris to explain his method.

"First I put my coins in groups," he began. "I put the pennies in one group, the nickels in a group, and the dimes in a group. Then I counted the pennies and I got sixteen. Then I counted the dimes: ten, twenty, thirty. Then I counted the nickels by fives and got fifteen." Chris stopped and fell silent.

"What did you do then?" I asked.

"I didn't figure out how much in all," he confessed, looking a little embarrassed.

"That's OK," I told him. "You have a good start. What can you do now?"

On the board, I wrote:

16, 30, 15

"These are the totals you have so far," I reminded.

"Well, thirty and fifteen . . . thirty and ten is forty, and forty and five is forty-five," he explained.

On the board, I recorded his thinking like this:

16 + 30 + 15
40 + 5 = 45

Chris then said, "Forty-five plus ten [the ten in the sixteen] pennies is fifty-five. Now I have to add the rest of the pennies. Fifty-six, fifty-seven, fifty-eight, fifty-nine, sixty, sixty-one. It's sixty-one cents in all."

I finished recording his thinking on the board:

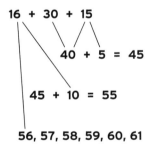

16 + 30 + 15
40 + 5 = 45
45 + 10 = 55
56, 57, 58, 59, 60, 61

"Who solved it a different way?" I asked.

"I made tens," Miguel reported. "First I took two nickels, and that's a ten. Then I added five pennies and a nickel, and that's another ten, so that makes twenty. Then I added three dimes, that's thirty, forty, fifty. Then I added ten pennies to make another ten; that's sixty. I added the last penny and got sixty-one, like Chris."

Rather than record Miguel's reasoning on the board as I had done for Chris, I modeled his thinking using coins so that the students could see Miguel's method in action. I continued to model this way for the remaining students who shared.

Nachelle went next. "I started with the nickels: five, ten, fifteen," she explained. "Then I added on the dimes: twenty-five, thirty-five, forty-five. I did the pennies last: forty-six, forty-seven, . . . sixty-one cents."

"I did it a different way," River said. "I started with the dimes: ten, twenty, thirty. Then I did the nickels: thirty-five, forty, forty-five. I finished with the pennies like Nachelle and got sixty-one cents, too."

I was impressed with the variety of ways in which these second graders approached the problem. Often, we tell students to start with the coins having the greatest value (in this case, the dimes) and work from there. This teaching strategy can preempt some creative problem solving by students. Allowing children to use strategies that make sense to them strengthens their problem-solving skills.

Extending the Activity

- Ask students to find the total value of a different collection of coins.
- Use coins made especially for the overhead projector to assist in teaching.
- Set up a learning center where students can work independently or with a partner to sort, count, and find the total value of a collection of coins.

Comparing Polygons

For Grades K-2

Overview

Geometry is a topic in mathematics that often takes a backseat to number and operations in many textbooks. Students typically learn about geometry for a few short weeks during the school year; this isn't nearly enough time to develop spatial sense and explore the properties of different figures. Therefore, incorporating math activities that focus on geometry is crucial.

In this activity, students are asked to compare two different polygons (many-sided, closed figures with straight line segments). By discussing how the two polygons are the same and different, students begin to build vocabulary that they can use to describe the attributes of other geometric shapes.

Activity Directions

1. Draw two different polygons on the board.
2. Underneath the polygons, draw a two-column chart.
3. Ask students to share with a partner how the two figures are the same and how they are different.
4. Lead a class discussion to elicit ideas from students. Record their ideas on the two-column chart.

Key Questions

- What's the name of this polygon?
- What's the same about these two polygons?
- What's different about these two polygons?
- Where do you see these polygons in the world? In the classroom?

CONTENT AREA

Geometry

MATERIALS

- optional: overhead projector

TIME

ten minutes

From the Classroom

As Shawn Yoshimoto's students filed in from recess and were settling into their seats, I drew two polygons on the board at the front of the room. Underneath the polygons, I drew a two-column chart and wrote the words *Same* and *Different* at the top:

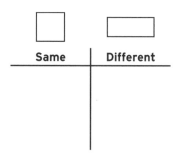

"What's the name of this polygon?" I asked, pointing to the square. The students responded in unison; they seemed confident that the polygon was a square.

"And this polygon?" I asked, pointing to the rectangle. Together, the class identified the polygon.

"Look at these two polygons," I then said, pointing to both the square and the rectangle. "Think about what is the same about the polygons and what is different about them. For example, I'm different than Mrs. Yoshimoto because I'm a man and she's a woman. We're the same because we're both people."

After about thirty seconds of think time, I directed the students to share their thoughts with a partner before calling for their attention. When the students settled, I asked them how the polygons were the same.

"They both have four corners," Demonte observed.

As I wrote *four corners* in the Same column of the chart, I told the students that mathematicians call the corners *angles*. We then counted the four angles on the square and then on the rectangle. As we counted, I pointed to the angles with my index finger. I wrote the word *angles* in parentheses next to the word *corners*:

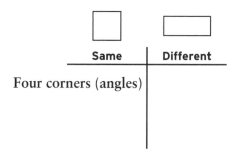

"They both have four sides," Osman said. After Osman reported his observation, we counted the sides on each polygon. As I had done with the angles, I pointed to the polygons' sides as we counted, intent on being as explicit as possible about where the sides were located. Then I recorded his idea on the chart. Xitlalic went next.

"If you cut the square in half, both sides are the same size. It's the same for the rectangle."

"You mean like this?" I asked her, dividing each polygon in half vertically, using a dotted line:

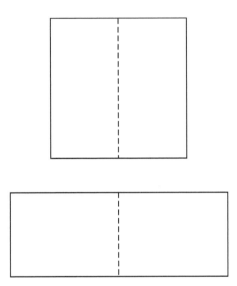

Xitlalic nodded her head in agreement.

I then asked the class, "Does anyone know what mathematicians call it when a polygon is divided in half so that each side is exactly the same shape and size?"

"Isn't the line that cuts the shapes in half called the line of symmetry?" Kierra asked. Shawn and I looked at one another, surprised and impressed with Kierra's knowledge.

"Yes," I confirmed, pointing to the vertical line of symmetry on both polygons. "Polygons can also have horizontal and diagonal lines of symmetry, too," I added, using my index finger to trace where the other lines of symmetry would be on the square and the rectangle. I also noted, with a light touch, that the square had vertical, horizontal, and diagonal symmetry, whereas the other rectangle I drew on the chart (see page 40) had only vertical and horizontal symmetry.

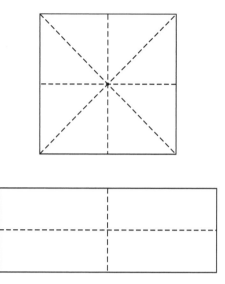

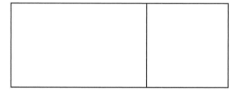

"I know how else the polygons are the same," Maria said. "You can make a square inside the rectangle."

"Come up and show us," I urged. Maria came up and drew a picture of a rectangle on the board next to the two-column chart. With chalk, she drew a vertical line from the top of the rectangle to the bottom, making a little square inside the rectangle.

Maria had identified an important idea in geometry: that shapes can be made from other shapes.

"Aren't rectangles and squares in the same family?" Kiana wondered aloud.

I waited a few seconds to see if anyone would respond to Kiana's question. When no one volunteered, I told the students that there are a few families to which squares and rectangles belong. Both are polygons (many-sided, closed shapes) and both are quadrilaterals (polygons with four sides). I also mentioned that both of these polygons are parallelograms—polygons that have two pairs of parallel lines. Finally, I noted that a square is a special type of rectangle.

We continued discussing the similarities and differences between the polygons until all of the students' ideas were exhausted. Our chart looked like this:

☐ Same	☐ Different
4 corners (angles)	rectangle has 2 equal sides;
4 sides	square has 4 equal sides
symmetrical	this square is smaller
quadrilaterals	this rectangle is longer
polygons	area of this rectangle is bigger
have vertical lines	perimeter of this rectangle is longer
have horizontal lines	they have different names
have parallel lines	

To complete the activity, I asked the students where they might see rectangles and squares in the classroom or in the world around them. Responses included the following:

"The cover of a book is a rectangle."
"The front of the door is a rectangle."
"There are squares on the ceiling of the classroom."
"The bases on the baseball field are square."
"The rug is rectangle shaped."

Extending the Activity

- Read the book *The Greedy Triangle*, by Marilyn Burns (1994), to complement the activity.
- Use a different pair of polygons for children to compare.
- Distribute two pattern blocks to pairs of students, and ask them to compare the shapes. This provides a hands-on experience that allows students to touch the shapes' sides, angles, and lines of symmetry.

7

Cubes in a Tube

For Grades K-2

CONTENT AREA

Algebra

MATERIALS

■ 20 interlocking
cubes, such as
Multilink, Snap, or
Unifix cubes,
snapped into a train
■ 1 sheet of 18-inch
newsprint

TIME

five minutes (ten to
fifteen minutes to in-
troduce the activity
on the first day)

Overview

In this activity, students gain experiences with identifying, describing, and extending patterns by predicting the color pattern of a cube train that is hidden inside a roll of newsprint.

There are two different types of patterns that young children should explore: repeating patterns and growing patterns. Repeating patterns involve the cyclical repetition of an identifiable unit. For example, in a *clap, snap, clap, snap, clap, snap* pattern, the *clap, snap* unit, or *core*, is repeated over and over. Repeating patterns have predictability built into them.

Growth patterns are also predictable. For example, in the *clap, snap, clap, clap, snap, clap, clap, clap, snap* pattern, the number of snaps stays constant while the number of claps grows by one more each time. Our system of counting is also a growing pattern; the consecutive numbers increase (or decrease) by a constant difference of one.

Children's early experiences with patterns should focus on recognizing regularity, identifying the same pattern in different forms, and using patterns to make predictions.

Activity Directions

1. Using interlocking cubes, make a cube train that has either a repeating or a growing pattern. The train should be ten, fifteen, or twenty cubes in length—not too short and not too long.
2. Make a tube just long enough to hide the cube train by rolling up a piece of 18-inch newsprint and taping it together so that it doesn't unroll. Hide the cube train inside.
3. Show the tube with the train hidden inside to the students. Ask them to predict what color they think the first cube will be and have them share their predictions.
4. After students share their predictions, reveal the color of the first cube.

5. Repeat Step 4 for each cube in the train until you have removed the entire train from the tube.
6. Show the students the cube train and have them make observations about the pattern.

Key Questions

- What color do you think the first cube will be?
- What do you think the color of the next cube will be? Why?
- What do you notice about the pattern?
- What part of the pattern is staying the same?
- What part of the pattern is changing?

From the Classroom

Day 1

I held up a tube made from a rolled-up piece of newsprint, 18 inches in length, for Elisabeth Frausto's students to see. Hidden inside the paper tube was a train of fifteen Snap Cubes that were arranged in a repeating AB pattern:

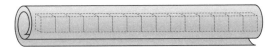

"Inside this paper tube are cubes snapped together to make a train," I began. "What color do you think the first cube will be?"

The students offered a variety of guesses: green, blue, red, and so on. When they were finished guessing, I slowly revealed the first cube, which was red. The students were excited.

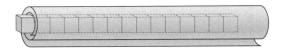

"What do you think the color of the next cube will be? What's your prediction?" I asked.

Again, the students offered a variety of predictions.

"Do we know for sure what color the next cube will be, or do we need more information?" I asked. Several students asked to see the next cube, so I slowly pulled the train from the paper tube, revealing a blue cube.

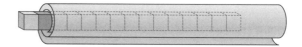

After seeing the blue cube, about half of the children predicted that the third cube would be red, making me think that they'd had some experience with AB patterns. Once I revealed the third cube and the students saw that it was red, they became animated.

"It's a pattern!" Miles exclaimed.

"How do you know?" I asked him.

"It goes red, blue, then red," he replied. "That's a pattern."

I continued to pull cubes from the tube, each time asking students to predict before I revealed the color. After I had shown eight cubes, the students were pretty confident they'd figured out the *core* of the pattern, or the part of the pattern that repeated over and over. Together, we "read" the pattern aloud while I pointed to each of the eight cubes that were sticking out from the paper tube.

"Red, blue, red, blue, red, blue, red, blue!" the students chorused.

When all the cubes were revealed, I asked a volunteer to hold up the cube train. While the students read the AB pattern aloud, I represented the pattern on the board using letters:

R B R B R B R B R B R B R B

Representing the pattern in different ways helps students recognize pattern structures in different contexts. In this case, the red-blue pattern can be represented with colored cubes or using symbolic notation (letters).

To help the students see the AB pattern in a different context, I asked them if they could line up in a girl-boy pattern that would match the pattern made with the colored cube train. The students were enthusiastic and wanted to try. With a little help, the class formed a line on the rug—first a girl, then a boy, and so on to represent the AB repeating pattern.

"How is lining up in a girl-boy pattern the same as the red-blue pattern we made with the cubes?" I asked. This question was important in helping students make the connection between the two patterns.

"It's like the reds are the girls and the blues are the boys!" Maria observed. "It goes red, blue, red, blue and we go girl, boy, girl, boy!"

Day 2

To continue the activity, I showed the students a paper tube with a new cube train hidden inside. This cube train was made with twenty connected cubes. Instead of creating a repeating pattern, I made a train with a growing pattern: white, brown, white, white, brown, white, white, white, brown, white, white, white, white, brown, and so on.

As with the repeating pattern in our first cube train, students guessed the color of each cube as I slowly revealed one cube at a time from the tube. Once the class had guessed the pattern and I had revealed the entire cube train, I held it up for everyone to see and make observations.

"It's a pattern," Gabriella said. "There's always one brown cube between the white ones."

"So we know from the pattern that there's going to be one brown cube between the white cubes," I said, paraphrasing Gabriella's idea. "What else do you notice?" I asked.

"It goes one, two, three, four, five!" exclaimed Ray.

"Which cubes are you counting, Ray?" I asked, pushing him to clarify.

"The white ones," he responded. "It starts with one white, then two whites, then three whites, four whites, then five whites."

When Ray finished explaining, I repeated what he'd said, pointing to the white cubes in the cube train so that students could see.

"Anything else?" I asked.

"There are five brown cubes in all," Lizette observed.

We counted the brown cubes together to check Lizette's idea. Finally, I recorded the pattern on the board and we read it aloud together:

W B W W B W W W B W W W W B W W W W W B

"What stays the same in the pattern?" I asked.

"There's always one brown cube," Nico said.

I then asked, "So what changes in the pattern?"

This question was difficult for the students, so I rephrased it.

"Nico said there's always just one brown," I said. "And Ray said something about how the white cubes start at one, then two, then three," I hinted. "So what changes in the pattern?" A few students' hands shot up.

"The whites keep getting more," Miles said.

"So the pattern changes when the white cubes increase," I paraphrased.

To finish the activity, I asked, "What do you think will come next in the pattern?" This question prompted students to make a prediction about the pattern if it were extended.

Extending the Activity

- On subsequent days, hide cube trains with different patterns, using different colors. For example, there are various repeating patterns to make, including AB patterns, AAB patterns, ABB patterns, ABC patterns, and ABCC patterns. As well, there are numerous growing patterns to make for students.

- Create a cube train pattern and then direct students to make a copy of it using their own cubes.
- Direct students to individually create their own "cubes in a tube" train pattern, and have their partner make predictions and describe the pattern.
- After students have figured out the core of the pattern, have them predict the color of the tenth cube, the fifteenth cube, or the twentieth cube in the pattern.

Dots

For Grades K-2

Overview

In this activity, children are presented with different arrangements of dots and asked to determine the total number of dots in each arrangement.

Counting is fundamental to basic number sense and includes more than knowing numbers' names, their sequence, and how to write them. Counting involves knowing that the number of objects does not change when the objects are moved, rearranged, or concealed. To count correctly, children need to know that as they count, each object they count has a particular number name. Counting also involves knowing that the last number named represents the last object and the last number counted represents the total number of objects. Learning to count takes time and happens as a result of many experiences. *Dots* is an activity that can help children learn to count quantities.

Students will use a variety of strategies when counting dots. Some will count all of the dots one by one to determine the total. Others will "see" a small number of dots without having to count them and then count on from there. Still other students will make the connection between dot patterns and number combinations by seeing the total number of dots as the sum of smaller parts (four dots and two dots and four more dots), not just as a group of single dots.

Counting dots can help children visualize quantities; they learn that the number 10 can stand for 10 discrete objects, or that 10 can be seen as 2 groups of 5 or 2 groups of 4 and 2 more, and so on. Learning to group numbers in different ways helps children develop effective strategies for adding and subtracting numbers.

Activity Directions

1. Show students an arrangement of dots.
2. Ask: "How many dots? How do you know?"
3. Repeat Steps 1 and 2.

CONTENT AREA

Number and Operations

MATERIALS

- dot arrangements, 1 set per student (see Blackline Masters and examples in vignette)

TIME

five to ten minutes

Key Question

• How many dots? How do you know?

From the Classroom

Frannie MacKenzie's students were seated on the rug in the front of the room. I began the activity by having the students practice answering questions using a whisper voice.

"We're going to start a new class activity called *Dots*," I began. "I'm going to draw some dots on the board. As soon as you know how many dots I've drawn, I want you to say the answer using a whisper voice."

We practiced saying "two," "three," "four," and "five" together in a quiet, choral voice. Then I drew two dots on the board like this:

●

●

All the students whispered, "Two." I then drew four dots in this configuration:

● ●

● ●

The students whispered, "Four," immediately.

"You didn't need to count them, did you?" I said. "You knew there were two right away, and then you knew there were four, just like that!" I exclaimed, snapping my fingers.

Next, I drew three dots on the board this way:

● ● ●

Again, the students knew the answer immediately and were delighted with themselves. One boy called out, "Do harder ones!" I nodded my head and smiled.

I then drew five dots in the familiar dice configuration:

● ●

●

● ●

Most students recognized the arrangement of five dots right away. I asked them if they'd used dice before, and students nodded and excitedly raised their hands.

"OK, ready for the next one?" I asked, focusing their attention on the board. I drew six dots like this:

$$
\begin{array}{ccc}
\bullet & \bullet & \bullet \\[4pt]
\bullet & \bullet & \\[4pt]
\bullet & &
\end{array}
$$

This time, no one had an immediate response. This dot arrangement seemed unfamiliar to the students. Perhaps if the grouping had been arranged like that on a die, some students might have recognized the amount right away. Typically, young children can perceive small amounts like two, three, four, and five without having to count. Six dots, at least in this arrangement, required some mathematical thinking on their part. I asked for volunteers to tell how many and explain how they knew. I called on Carlos.

"It's six."

"Come up and show us, Carlos," I said. Carlos walked to the board.

"There's three," he said, pointing to the vertical column of three dots. "Four, five," he continued, counting on the next vertical column of two dots. "And six," he concluded, counting the last dot. Carlos started with a small amount that he recognized without counting (three) and then counted on. This is a mathematical leap from having to count each dot individually.

"Did anyone think about it differently?" I asked.

"I counted by twos," Betina announced. She walked up to the board and confidently counted the dots by twos, touching pairs of dots as she counted. I thanked her and had the class practice Betina's strategy, counting the dots by twos as I touched pairs of dots with my fingers. I deliberately pointed to each pair of dots because I know that when students first learn to say a particular skip-counting sequence (two, four, six, eight, . . .), they may not yet recognize that each successive number in the sequence represents the addition of a particular quantity. Activities such as counting dots help students connect the numbers in the counting sequence to the quantities they represent.

For the final dot arrangement, I drew ten dots like this:

$$
\begin{array}{ccccc}
\bullet & \bullet & \bullet & \bullet & \bullet \\[4pt]
\bullet & \bullet & \bullet & \bullet & \bullet
\end{array}
$$

Students shared a variety of strategies for finding the total number of dots: counting by ones, twos, and fives. Sarah said that she saw "four plus two plus four." As she described her strategy, I circled dots in this way to help make her thinking visible:

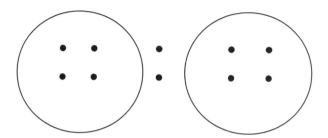

Students like Sarah are just beginning to recognize connections between dot patterns and number combinations (e.g., $4 + 2 + 4 = 10$).

Extending the Activity

Dots is an activity that can be used throughout the school year. You may want to extend the activity by drawing more difficult arrangements such as these (see Blackline Masters for more dot arrangements):

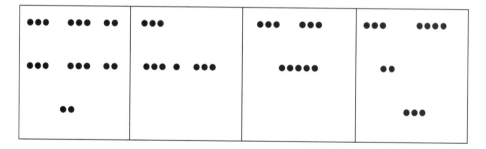

To assist children in learning to recognize sets of objects in patterned arrangements without having to count, consider drawing dot arrangements on paper plates. Hold up a "dot plate" for only one to three seconds. Ask, "How many? How did you see it?" Students can also use the dot plates as a partner activity during math time.

Estimating

For Grades K–2

Overview

Estimating is an important skill that helps students develop their number sense. In this activity, students first estimate and then count how many cubes there are inside someone's hand or in a glass jar. Using concrete objects to estimate and count helps children visualize the quantities that numbers represent.

The *Estimating* activity for kindergarten and first grade focuses students' learning on the concepts of more and less, counting, and estimating quantities up to twenty. The activity provides second graders with the opportunity to think about place value and our base ten number system by having them consider how many groups of ten there are in the number twenty-four (or whatever the total number of cubes happens to be).

Activity Directions for Grades K-1

1. Show students a small amount of cubes and ask them how many there are.
2. Ask a student to take a handful of cubes from a plastic bag full of cubes.
3. Ask the students to estimate how many cubes there are in the handful. Record their estimates on the board.
4. Count the cubes to determine the total.
5. Have a second student take a handful from the bag. Ask the other students if the second handful will be larger or smaller than the first. Count the cubes and compare the totals.
6. Finally, take a handful, put the cubes in trains of five, and ask the students to count the cubes. If necessary, help them count the cubes.

Key Questions

- About how many cubes do you think _____ can hold in his hand?
- This is what a handful of cubes looks like. Now how many cubes do you think _____ can hold in his hand?

CONTENT AREA

Number and Operations

MATERIALS

- plastic bag (grades K–1), glass jar (grade 2)
- 20–40 interlocking cubes, such as Multilink, Snap, or Unifix cubes

TIME

ten minutes

- What can help you make a good estimate?
- Do you think _____ (second student) can pick up more or fewer cubes than _____ (first student)?
- How many more cubes did _____ pick up than _____?

Activity Directions for Grade 2

1. Show the students a jar filled with cubes.
2. Ask the students to estimate how many cubes there are in the jar. Record their estimates on the board.
3. Show students ten cubes and ask them if they want to change their estimates.
4. Count the cubes in the jar by ones, then twos, and then fives, asking students whether the number of cubes will stay the same or change each time.
5. Determine how many groups of tens and ones are in the jar.

Key Questions

- About how many cubes do you think there are in this jar?
- How can we find out how many cubes there are?
- What if we count by twos (or fives or tens)? Will there still be __ (total number) cubes? Explain.
- This is what ten cubes looks like. Now how many cubes do you think there are inside the jar?
- If I took the cubes out of the jar and snapped them together in trains of ten cubes each, how many trains of ten would I have? How many extras would there be? Explain.
- What if there were forty-five cubes in the jar? How many trains of ten? How many extra? Explain.

From a Kindergarten and First-Grade Classroom

The kindergartners and first graders in Elisabeth Frausto's class sat in a circle on the rug at the front of the room, looking excited and ready to learn.

"We'll be estimating and counting this morning," I announced. I then grabbed three cubes from a plastic bag, placed them on the rug in the middle of the circle, and asked the students how many cubes they saw.

"Three!" the students chorused.

"That was easy, huh?" I said. "You didn't even need to count them."

I then asked Justin to use one hand to grab a handful of cubes from the bag and show the handful to the students.

"Does anyone know how many cubes Justin is holding?" I asked.

"There's too many; we have to count them," Kent replied.

"Let's estimate first," I said. "Take a look at the cubes in Justin's hand. About how many do you think he's holding?"

I gave the students some time to think and then I asked them to whisper their estimates to a partner before reporting to the class.

"I think he's holding six," Gabe guessed.

"Maybe ten," Areysi said.

"I think fifteen," David added.

As the students continued to report, I recorded the different estimates on the board:

6   10   15   18   12   14   11   13

"I don't have a guess," Emme said. "But the cubes are fat and they take up a lot on his hand."

"Does that help you make an estimate?" I asked. I was impressed with Emme's reasoning.

"Yes," she answered.

"What else can help you make a good estimate?" I asked the class.

"Maybe the color of the cubes," Michael said.

"Maybe if you just count a few in his hand, it can help you make a guess," added Tiara.

It was interesting to listen to students' ideas; some made mathematical sense while others didn't. With experience, the students would begin to make estimates based on sound reasoning, like the size or shape of what was being measured, rather than on something arbitrary, like color.

Next, I asked Justin to spill the cubes onto the rug.

"Let's count the cubes together," I told the class. As I touched one cube at a time, the students counted with me. Altogether, Justin had picked up fourteen cubes.

"Your estimates were pretty good!" I exclaimed.

Next, I asked Kiara to grab a handful of cubes from the bag. As she held up the cubes, I asked the students whether they thought Kiara could hold more or fewer cubes than Justin. Most students thought that Justin could hold more.

After Kiara placed her cubes on the rug, the students counted with me. Altogether, Kiara had picked up twelve cubes.

"How many more cubes did Justin pick up than Kiara?" I asked. This question stumped the class. After I waited about twenty seconds, there still was no response, so I asked the students to count Kiara's cubes with me again. Once we got to twelve, I reached into the bag and added two more cubes to get fourteen. This made it easier for students to see that Justin's handful exceeded Kiara's by just two cubes.

After putting Kiara's cubes back into the bag, I reached in and grabbed a handful. I showed the students my cubes and asked them to estimate about how many cubes were in my hand. Students' estimates ranged from seven to one hundred.

Rather than spill the cubes onto the rug as Justin and Kiara had, I carefully placed them in rows of five cubes each. I then asked the class how many cubes were on the rug, thinking that someone might count by fives to find the total. Instead of counting by fives, everyone was busy trying to count the cubes by ones and having a difficult time keeping track of his or her count.

"Let's count the cubes together," I suggested. As I touched the cubes one by one, the students counted out twenty-one cubes.

"Raise your hand if you can count by fives," I said. Most students indicated that they could. We then counted the cubes together by fives while I pointed to each group as we counted to help students connect the counting sequence with the quantities being counted.

From a Second-Grade Classroom

"About how many cubes do you think there are in this jar?" I asked Robin Gordon's class of second graders, who were gathered on the rug in front of me. I was holding a glass jar with twenty-four Snap Cubes inside. Several students immediately raised their hands.

"I want to give you some think time, so put your hands down, please," I told the class. "Think about how many cubes there are in the jar and make an estimate." I waited for about thirty seconds, and then I directed the students to turn to a partner and share their ideas. Giving the class an opportunity to have a partner talk allows more students to communicate their thinking.

"Attention back on me on zero," I directed. "Five, four, three, two, one, zero. Eyes up here." This countdown helped refocus students' attention.

"Raise your hand if you'd like to share your estimate," I said. Almost everyone raised a hand. As each student reported his or her estimate, I wrote the number on the whiteboard. When students were finished, I'd written these numbers on the board:

10   28   25   11   40   16   12   15   30   13   14   18   19   22

"Take a look at your estimates," I said. "Which number is the largest?" I waited until many hands were in the air, then I called on Tamika.

"Forty is the biggest number," she said.

"And what about the smallest number?" I asked the class.

"Ten is the smallest," David reported. I wrote the word *range* below the students' estimates and then wrote:

The smallest estimate is 10 and the greatest estimate is 40.
The range is 30.

"Mathematicians would say that the range of your estimates is ten to forty," I said. "Ten is the smallest estimate and forty is the greatest. There are thirty numbers between ten and forty, so the range is thirty."

"What if I said to you that I think there are two hundred cubes inside the jar? Would that be a good estimate or not?" I asked this question to get the students to consider the idea of reasonableness.

"No!" they responded. Several students giggled.

"That's way too many," Monica asserted. "It's a lot less than that."

"What if I guessed three cubes?" I asked.

"That's way too small," Sol responded. "I can even count up to three in there—I can see them."

"So some estimates are good ones and some aren't. Some are reasonable and some are unreasonable," I clarified. "Your estimates look pretty good to me."

I then asked the class how we could find out the exact number of cubes inside the jar, and several students suggested that we count them.

"First I'm going to take ten cubes out of the jar and then have you rethink your estimate." I asked Mark to come stand next to me as I counted out ten cubes, one by one, placing them in his hand. The class counted with me.

"Here are ten cubes," I said, pointing to the cubes in Mark's hand. "And the rest are inside the jar."

"The jar is about half full now," Miguel commented.

"Now think about how many cubes the jar holds," I said. Instead of recording new estimates on the board, I asked the students whether they wanted to increase their estimate, decrease their estimate, or stick with their original guess. I also asked if anyone was unsure about what to do.

Some students wanted to change their estimates while others chose to stick with their original guesses.

Next, we counted the remaining cubes in the jar. The students were excited to find out that the jar held twenty-four cubes in all.

"What if we count the cubes by twos? Will we still have twenty-four cubes? What do you think?" I asked this question to see whether students could conserve number—that is, whether they understood that no matter how we counted the twenty-four cubes (by ones, twos, fives, tens, and so on), the total number would not change. This is an important idea for children to understand.

"Yes," Sol said. "It's the same thing if you count by ones or twos or fives. The number won't change."

"I think there will be more, 'cause you're counting by twos," Miguel countered.

"Let's find out," I said. I then took two cubes at a time and placed them back in the jar as the class counted with me. When we were finished counting, there were still twenty-four cubes in the jar. Miguel looked puzzled.

"How about if we count the cubes by fives?" I asked, pushing a little further on students' thinking.

"We'll still have twenty-four," River said. "It doesn't matter."

I then proceeded to count out five cubes at a time as the class counted along: "Five, ten, fifteen, twenty."

"What about the rest?" I asked, pointing to the four cubes remaining in the jar.

"Count those by ones," suggested Tamika.

After we determined that counting by fives would also yield a total of twenty-four, I put the cubes back into the jar. I then asked the class another question.

"There are twenty-four cubes inside the jar, right?" I said as I wrote the number *24* on the whiteboard. Students nodded their heads in agreement.

"If I took the cubes out of the jar and snapped them together in trains of ten cubes each, how many trains of ten would I have? And how many extras would there be?"

I gave the children some time to ponder this question before having them share their thinking. Of the students who volunteered their ideas, all of them stated that there would be two trains of ten and four extras, referring to the digits in the number 24 as clues that helped them. This type of reasoning signals an understanding of place value.

To finish the lesson, I snapped the cubes together and confirmed that we could indeed make two trains of ten with four extras. I left the students with the following questions to think about: "What if there were forty-five cubes in the jar? How many trains of ten? How many extra? What about fifty-four cubes?"

Extending the Activity for Grade 2

- Change the number of cubes in the jar.
- Start with an empty jar and ask how many cubes the jar could hold.
- Use a different-sized jar.
- Use different counters, such as pennies, beans, or marbles.

10

Finding Friendly Numbers

For Grade 2

CONTENT AREA

Number and
Operations

MATERIALS

■ none

TIME

ten to fifteen minutes

Overview

In this activity, students mentally estimate the answer to a story problem before finding the exact answer. First, they compute using friendly numbers. Next, students figure the exact answer to the problem, and finally they compare it with their estimates.

Friendly numbers, or landmark numbers, are familiar numbers used to make simple estimates or calculations. For example, numbers that are rounded to the nearest ten or five are easier to work with when adding or subtracting ($50 - 25$ is easier than $53 - 27$).

Activity Directions

1. Write a story problem on the board and have students read it aloud.
2. Ask students to talk with a partner about what they know and what they need to find out in order to solve the story problem.
3. With the class, identify the numbers and operations needed in order to solve the problem.
4. Guide the students in identifying friendly numbers that can be used in place of the numbers in the story problem. For example, a friendly number for fifty-three might be fifty, and a friendly number for twenty-seven might be twenty-five.
5. Direct students to make initial estimates using the friendly numbers identified (e.g., $50 - 25$).
6. Have students find the exact answer to the story problem and compare it with their estimates.

Key Questions

- What do we know about the problem?
- What do we need to find out to solve the problem?
- What does it mean to *make an estimate*? Explain.

- What is a *friendly number*? Explain.
- What friendly number could we use for __?

From the Classroom

I asked Robin Gordon's second graders to read aloud with me the story problem I had written on the board:

Fifty-three students were eating lunch.
Twenty-seven students left to go play.
How many students were still eating in the cafeteria?

"I want you to think about the story problem and then talk with a partner and tell one another what you know and what you need to find out to solve the problem." Robin's class was used to this exercise. She told me that she wanted her students to think about and reflect on problems first before performing any operations.

"What do we know?" I asked the students after giving them a few minutes to talk to each other.

"We know that there are fifty-three students who were eating lunch at first," Kay said.

"What do you mean by *at first*?" I asked her.

"Well, some of them left to go play," she responded.

"How many left to go play?" I asked.

"Twenty-seven!" several students replied.

"So we know that at first there were fifty-three students. Then twenty-seven left to go play. What do we need to find out?" I asked. Lots of hands went up. I called on Sol.

"We need to figure out how many are still eating lunch."

"That's correct, Sol. Today, we're going to start by estimating how many students were still eating lunch," I told the students. "Then we'll figure the exact answer. Who can tell us what it means to make an estimate?"

"It's like a guess," Jasmine said.

"That's right. An estimate is a guess. But in math, we try to make good estimates or guesses so that it's close to the exact answer. One way to help us make a good estimate is to use *friendly numbers*. Who can explain to us what a friendly number is?" The students seemed stumped by my question, so I decided to provide some support. I wrote these two equations on the board:

71 + 32   or   70 + 30

"Which one is easier to solve?" I asked.

"Seventy plus thirty," Eduardo said. "It's easy; all you have to do is count by tens."

"So seventy and thirty are friendly numbers because they're easier to work with," I explained.

"Let's look back at our problem," I said, pointing to the story problem on the board:

Fifty-three students were eating lunch.
Twenty-seven students left to go play.
How many students were still eating in the cafeteria?

"We know that fifty-three and twenty-seven are the numbers we have to work with," I reminded. "Let's think about what operation we want to use. Tell a partner what operation you would use to solve the problem and why." I knew the students were familiar with the word *operation*. Otherwise, I would have used the term along with examples such as addition, subtraction, multiplication, and division.

"Attention back up here," I directed. "Which operation should we use?"

"I think it's a subtraction problem," Cindy said. "You start with fifty-three, and twenty-seven leave, so you take twenty-seven away." When Cindy was finished sharing her idea, I wrote this equation on the board:

$53 - 27 =$

"Other ideas?" No one raised a hand. There are often many different strategies one can use to solve math problems. This problem is no exception. For example, students could use addition to solve the problem: $27 + \_\_\_ = 53$. But since the focus of the lesson was on finding friendly numbers, I didn't spend time pushing for different methods.

"Let's look at the number fifty-three. Can anyone think of a friendly number for fifty-three?" No responses were forthcoming, so I quickly drew a number line on the board like this:

50 51 52 53 54 55 56 57 58 59 60

I then asked, "Is there a friendly number for fifty-three that you can see on the number line?" This time, lots of students raised their hands. I called on River.

"I think fifty is friendly 'cause you can count by tens," he explained.

"I think fifty-five 'cause fives are easy for me," Michael added.

"Maybe sixty 'cause you can count by tens using sixty, too," Isaiah said.

"What about the other number in our problem, twenty-seven?" I quickly sketched another number line on the board, but this one had empty spaces so that the students would have an opportunity to think about the relative positions of the numbers.

<u>20   27   30</u>

"What are some friendly numbers for twenty-seven?" I asked. This time, it took a few seconds before students began to raise their hands.

"Where's twenty-five on the number line?" Isaiah asked.

"Good question," I replied. "Where do you think? Would it go closer to twenty, twenty-seven, or thirty?"

"It's close to the twenty-seven, a little bit that way," he said, pointing to the left of the 27. I wrote *25* on the number line as Isaiah had explained:

<u>20   25   27   30</u>

"I think twenty-five is a friendly number for twenty-seven 'cause it's close to twenty-seven," Maria said.

"I think thirty is friendly, too," Michael added.

"What about twenty?" Jose asked.

"Twenty, twenty-five, and thirty are all friendly numbers because they're easy to work with when you add or subtract," I told the class. "But I would use twenty-five or thirty rather than twenty in this problem because twenty-five and thirty are closer to twenty-seven."

Next, I wrote the friendly numbers for fifty-three and twenty-seven that the students had identified:

50   55   60   20   25   30

Together, we used different combinations of these numbers to make some estimates for the answer to the story problem. For example, students solved for $50 - 20$, $50 - 25$, $50 - 30$, $55 - 20$, $60 - 20$, and so on to make various estimates.

Finally, to complete the activity, we determined the exact answer to the problem: $53 - 27 = 26$. Then we compared the exact answer with students' estimates to see which estimate was closest to twenty-six.

Extending the Activity

Pose a different addition or subtraction story problem each day you teach this activity. Story problems should include multidigit numbers that are not friendly numbers (e.g., 43 + 27 or 123 − 41).

Fit the Facts

For Grades K–2

11

CONTENT AREA

Number and Operations

MATERIALS

- *Fit the Facts* family letters, 1 per student (see Blackline Masters)
- chart paper

TIME

five to ten minutes (fifteen minutes to introduce the activity on the first day)

Overview

In this activity, students play a matching game called *Fit the Facts*. To begin, students are shown a list of three numbers. The teacher writes on the board a fact, or piece of information, that goes with one of the three numbers. The students match the fact with its number. The process is repeated until all three numbers have been used. Your age, the number of siblings you have, and the number of pets you have are examples of personal facts and numbers that can be used to introduce this activity. The students then receive a homework assignment, the *Fit the Facts* family letter, in which they generate their own personal facts and numbers. Students bring the homework assignment back to class for the teacher to use in subsequent matching games.

The activity helps children learn that numbers can be used in a variety of ways, including to quantify, to measure, and to locate. Seeing the usefulness of numbers and knowing that certain numbers make sense in some situations and not in others are important aspects of number sense.

Activity Directions for Day 1

1. Ask the students where they see numbers in the world around them and record their ideas on chart paper.
2. On the board, write three numbers that have some significance in your life. For example:

   your age
   the number of sisters and/or brothers you have
   the number of pets you have

3. Write a sentence that gives a clue for each number and ask students to match each sentence with one of the numbers.

   I am __ years old.
   I have __ sisters.
   I have __ pets.

4. Send home copies of the *Fit the Facts* family letter for students and families to complete and return.

Activity Directions for Subsequent Days

1. Choose a student's paper from the collection of *Fit the Facts* family letters that students returned from home.
2. Record the student's numbers on the board and have the class practice reading the numbers aloud.
3. Write a sentence (see the *Fit the Facts* family letter in the Blackline Masters) on the board that provides a clue for one of the student's numbers. Then have the class determine which number fits in the blank. Continue writing sentences and playing the matching game. For example:

> I am __ years old.
> I am in __ grade.
> I live at __.
> I am __ inches tall.

Key Questions

- Where do you see numbers in the world around you?
- Which number might fit the fact? Explain.
- What other numbers might fit the fact? Explain.
- Which numbers are unreasonable and won't fit the fact? Explain.

From the Classroom

Day 1

"Where do you see numbers in the world around you?" I asked Frannie MacKenzie's students.

"At the store," Betina said.

"In my house," John added.

"Where in your house?" I probed.

"Like on the clock," he responded. I wrote *store* and *clock* on a piece of chart paper titled "Numbers Around Us" and continued doing so as students offered ideas.

"How about the numbers on the stove in the kitchen," Sarah said.

"What are those numbers used for?" I asked her.

"They tell how hot it's going to get," she responded.

"Where else do you see numbers in the world?" I asked. The class got quiet.

"What about in the classroom? Where do you see numbers in here?" I asked. Soon lots of hands were wiggling in the air. The students now had plenty of ideas. They saw numbers on books, measuring tapes, bingo cards, class charts, and the computer.

When students were finished sharing their ideas, I told the class that we were going to play a matching game called *Fit the Facts*.

"These are my personal numbers," I told the class as I wrote the following three numbers on the whiteboard: *0, 48,* and *3.* Together we read the numbers aloud as I pointed to each one.

"Now I'm going to write sentences and you're going to match which numbers fit in the blanks, or fit the facts," I explained. "Here goes. Let's read the words together." On the board I wrote:

I am ___ years old.

"Which number fits in the fact?" I asked. "Which number would go in the blank? Think about it and then raise your hand if you know." Maureen raised her hand and guessed forty-eight.

"Would it make sense to put the number three in the blank?" I asked.

"No!" the class responded.

"That's too little!" someone said.

"What about zero? Does that make sense? Is that reasonable?" I asked. This prompted lots of giggles from the students. I wrote *48* to complete the sentence:

I am 48 years old.

Next, I wrote this sentence on the board:

I have ___ sisters.

This time, several students guessed three and some guessed zero. We agreed that both numbers could fit. I then told them that I have three sisters and wrote *3* to complete the sentence:

I have 3 sisters.

Next, I wrote the final sentence on the board:

I have ___ pets.

Everyone knew the answer since there were no other numbers left from which to choose, so I wrote the number *0* to complete the sentence:

I have 0 pets.

After the students had guessed my personal numbers, I showed the students the *Fit the Facts* family letter (see Blackline Masters) and explained the homework assignment to them. At the end of the day, Frannie distributed the letters.

Day 2

The next day I gathered students on the rug and collected the *Fit the Facts* family letters that had been returned. Frannie would continue to collect the rest of the letters throughout the week.

I leafed through the papers and selected Cody's to share with the class. I introduced Cody's numbers by writing them on the board, being careful not to put them in the same order as they appeared on the homework sheet:

100

7

6

49

1

1st

3833

$\frac{1}{2}$

1

As we read the numbers together, we stopped at ones that were a little tricky. For example, I told the class that 3833 would be read either as "three eight three three" or "thirty-eight thirty-three" rather than "three thousand eight hundred thirty-three." When we got to $\frac{1}{2}$, I probed to see if anyone could actually read the number.

"Is it twelve?" Victor wondered.

"How about twenty-one?" Monica asked.

"One and a half!" Tyron stated. He seemed sure of himself.

"That's really close, Tyron," I hinted.

"One-half!" he exclaimed.

I confirmed that he was correct and quickly provided some examples of one-half by folding a piece of paper in half, showing half of a pencil, designating where the halfway mark was on a coffee cup, and walking halfway across the rug.

I then proceeded to write one sentence on the board at a time, each time having students determine the missing number. After students had correctly matched a number, I wrote the number in the blank. Here's what the sentences looked like using all of Cody's numbers:

Cody's Numbers

I am <u>6</u> years old.
I am in <u>1st</u> grade.
I live at <u>3833</u> Front St.
I am <u>49</u> inches tall.
I live $\frac{1}{2}$ blocks away from school.
My favorite number is <u>100</u>.
I have <u>1</u> brother and <u>1</u> sister.
I have <u>7</u> pets.

As students guessed numbers, I posed questions that were designed to help the class think about reasonableness: "Would one-half fit for the number of brothers Cody has? Why not?" "Could Cody be six inches tall? Why not?" "Does one hundred fit the number of brothers Cody could have?" Some of Cody's statements could be answered with more than one number. For example, he could have had one pet rather than seven. Or he could have been seven years old rather than six.

Extending the Activity

Choose a different *Fit the Facts* family letter each day to share with the class, and play the matching game.

12

Greater Than, Less Than, Is Equal To

For Grades K–2

CONTENT AREA

Algebra

Number and Operations

MATERIALS

- interlocking cubes, such as Multilink, Snap, or Unifix cubes, about 20–30 per student

TIME

ten to fifteen minutes

Overview

Learning the meaning of the "less than," "greater than," and equals signs is important to children's algebraic understanding. Students need to understand that the equals sign means that the quantity on the left is the same as the quantity on the right (e.g., $4 + 5 = 3 + 6$). Students often think of the equals sign as an indicator that some action should take place. For example, when students with this misconception solve a problem like $3 + \_ = 7$, they add the 3 and the 7 and write *10* in the blank space.

Students benefit from experiences that require them to think about and discuss the meaning of symbols used in mathematics. In this activity, students use the "greater than," "less than," and equals signs to compare numbers and to compare sums.

Activity Directions

1. Have two students come to the front of the room and take turns grabbing a handful of cubes. As the two volunteers hold up their handfuls for the class to see, ask the students to estimate which handful has the most cubes or whether there are about the same number of cubes in each handful.

2. Draw outlines of two hands on the board and write the name of one student volunteer below one of the hands and the name of the other student volunteer below the other hand. Inside each hand, write the number of cubes each volunteer grabbed.

Victor   Maricela

3. Have each volunteer snap his or her cubes together into a tower, and then count and compare them.

4. Introduce the "greater than" sign (>), "less than" sign (<), and equals sign (=) to the class.

5. Introduce the following sentence frames:

___ is greater than ___.
___ is less than ___.
___ is equal to ___.

6. Together with the class, compare the student volunteers' numbers by using the appropriate sentence frame.

Additional Activity Directions for Grades 1 and 2

7. Repeat Steps 1–4 and 6, but instead of having the volunteers grab one handful each, have them grab two handfuls each. After the volunteers count the cubes in each of their handfuls, draw outlines of their hands on the board and have students compare the sums.

8. Pose "missing number" scenarios by drawing outlines of four hands so that one or more of the numbers in the handfuls are missing. Have students figure out which numbers are missing:

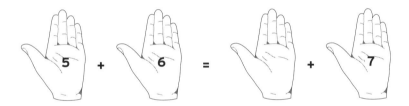

Key Questions

• Who do you think grabbed more cubes? Or do you think the two students grabbed the same, or an equal, number of cubes?

• How many more cubes did _____ grab than _____? How do you know?

• Did anyone solve the problem in a different way?

• Which sign should we record between the expressions—greater than, less than, or equal to?

From the Classroom

Sharon Fargason's students sat on the rug at the front of the room, watching as I held up a tub of Snap Cubes. I directed two student volunteers,

Maricela and Victor, to come up and grab one handful of cubes each from the tub. After they had grabbed their cubes, I asked them to hold up their handfuls for the class to see.

"Who do you think grabbed more cubes?" I asked. "Or do you think Maricela and Victor grabbed the same, or an equal, number of cubes?"

There was a mix of opinions; some thought that Victor had grabbed more cubes and some thought Maricela had grabbed more. To check, I asked Maricela and Victor to count their cubes. When they were finished, I drew outlines of two hands on the board. I labeled one hand *Victor* and the other hand *Maricela*. Next, I asked Victor to record the number 9 inside the hand with his name to represent his cubes, and then I directed Maricela to write the number 6 inside the hand with her name:

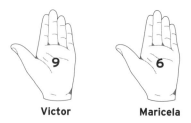

Victor   Maricela

"Who grabbed more cubes?" I asked the class.

"Victor!" the students exclaimed.

I then asked Victor and Maricela to each snap their cubes together to make a tower. I had them put their towers side by side to prove that Victor had more cubes.

"How many *more* cubes did Victor grab than Maricela?" I asked.

Having Victor and Maricela hold their towers next to each other made it easier for the class to compare quantities:

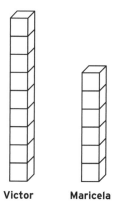

Victor   Maricela

"Three!" several students exclaimed.

"How do you know?" I asked.

I called on Oscar, who came up to the front and counted the extra three cubes in Victor's train that extended beyond Maricela's.

Next, I recorded the "greater than" sign between the 9 and the 6 like this:

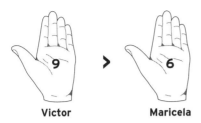

I pointed to the sign and said, "This is a shortcut way to write *greater than*. It looks to me like the mouth of an animal, opened wide, because it's hungry and wants to eat the amount that is greater."

Next, I wrote the "greater than" sign, the "less than" sign, and the equals sign on the board, listing different ways to describe the signs:

>	<	=
is more than	is less than	equals
is bigger than	is smaller than	is equal to
is greater than		is the same as

I then introduced the following sentence frames that students could use when comparing quantities:

___ is greater than ___.
___ is less than ___.
___ is equal to ___.

Together, we read aloud the sentence frames, pausing for the blank spaces. Then we used the frames to compare nine and six.

"Let's practice using one of the sentence frames to compare Maricela's cubes and Victor's cubes," I said.

In a choral voice, we read, "Nine is greater than six."

Over the next several days, Sharon continued the activity with her first graders, calling on different pairs of students to grab handfuls of cubes, count them, and compare the quantities using the "greater than," "less than," or equals sign and the sentence frames.

The Following Week

After students had several experiences comparing two handfuls, I returned to the class with a challenge. I wanted students to gain experience comparing quantities in a different way—this time, I would have them compare sums.

"Today we're going to grab handfuls of cubes, but this time we'll have volunteers grab two handfuls each instead of one."

Habrekka and Nith volunteered to grab two handfuls each. They counted the cubes in each handful and recorded the amounts in the hands I'd drawn on the board:

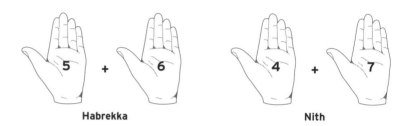

"Which is greater, the number of cubes Habrekka grabbed or the number of cubes Nith grabbed?" I asked. "Or are they equal amounts? Talk with a partner about what you think."

After several seconds, I asked for the students' attention and called on Jade.

"I think they are equal," she began. "Five plus six is eleven and four plus seven is eleven."

"How do you know that five and six is eleven?" I asked.

"'Cause I started with six and I counted five more: six, seven, eight, nine, ten, eleven," Jade said, demonstrating with her fingers.

"And four plus seven, how did you know that it is equal to eleven?" I asked.

"The same way. I started with four and went five, six, seven, eight, nine, ten, eleven; I counted on my fingers," Jade explained.

"Did anyone solve the problems in a different way?" I asked. After waiting a bit, I called on Justin.

"To figure out five plus six, I know that five and five is ten, so one more makes eleven," Justin explained. "And for four plus seven, I did it like Jade; I started with four and counted till I got to eleven," he continued, using his fingers to count on from four.

"How about another way?" I probed. "Did anyone figure it out *without* adding?"

Jose, an advanced math student, according to Sharon, came up to the board. He pointed to the numbers as he explained, "I know that five is one more than four, but six is one less than seven, so they are the same, equal."

Jose was thinking about the relationships between the numbers in the expression, an indicator that his algebraic thinking was well developed for his age.

When we were sure that 5 + 6 was equal to 4 + 7, I asked the students which sign to record between the expressions: <, >, or =.

I called on Nancy, who came up to the board and wrote an equals sign between 5 + 6 and 4 + 7:

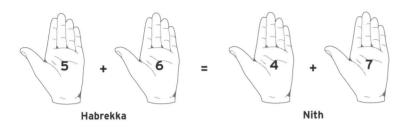

After Nancy had finished recording the sign, I directed the class to use one of the sentence frames to compare the sums. Together, we read aloud, "Five plus six is equal to four plus seven."

Later in the Year

Sharon Fargason's first graders had extensive prior experience with the activity *Greater Than, Less Than, Is Equal To* before I introduced an extension to the activity.

"Today we're going to look at a record of what happened when two students each grabbed two handfuls of cubes," I said, pointing to a drawing of the outlines of four hands I'd drawn on the board with numbers inside three of them:

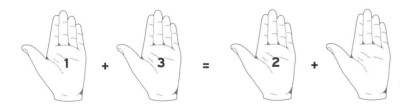

"The problem is that they forgot to write all the numbers and there's one blank handful," I explained. "I'd like you to figure out what number is missing."

I then distributed a train of twenty Snap Cubes to each student and told them that they could use the cubes if they needed them to solve the "missing number" problem.

I gave the students a little more than a minute to work on the problem and then asked for their attention and called on Nancy.

"The missing number is two," she said. "I didn't need my cubes, 'cause I know that one plus three is four and I know that two and two is four."

"I used my fingers," Cynthia explained. "I knew that one and three makes four, then I put up two fingers and counted two fingers until I got four."

"Raise your hand if you used your fingers to solve the problem," I said. Several hands went up. "Raise your hand if you solved it like Nancy, who just knew that two and two is four." A few hands went up.

"Any other ideas?" I asked. "Did anyone use their cubes?" No one raised a hand, so I posed another scenario by erasing the numbers inside the hands and recording new numbers:

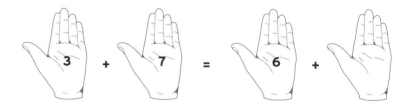

This time I gave students a little more time to work on the "missing number" problem and encouraged them to discuss their ideas with a partner.

While watching them work, I observed several students using their cubes. Jawrana snapped seven cubes together with three cubes and counted them by ones to arrive at a total of ten cubes. He then snapped six cubes together and put the tower next to the tower of ten. After looking at the two trains of cubes, Jawrana added four cubes to the smaller tower.

Some students counted on their fingers from six until they reached ten. A few students seemed to know the answer right away. After a few minutes, I called them back to attention and asked for their ideas.

Jose, who usually had a unique way of solving problems, went first. "I know that three and seven is ten, and I know that six and four makes ten," he explained. "I know my tens." A few students nodded in agreement.

"I think the answer is ten," Tracy said. "'Cause seven and three is ten."

This is a common mistake for children to make: they think that an answer should follow a computation, in this case, 3 + 7. Tracy's answer signaled that she did not understand the meaning of the equals sign. Instead of telling her that her idea was incorrect, I posed a question that would require Tracy to confront her misconception.

"Use your cubes," I told her. "Is six plus ten equal to three plus seven?"

As she worked with her cubes to find out, I thought about how important it is for teachers to guide children as they develop their own understanding of symbols like the equals sign.

Extending the Activity

Sharon continued to use this activity throughout the remainder of the school year. Eventually, Sharon stopped using illustrations of hands and used only equations for students to solve. Following are some examples of the "missing number" scenarios she posed:

$3 + 5 = 4 + \underline{}$ $4 + 1 = \underline{} + 5$

$6 + 3 = \underline{} + 4$ $\underline{} + 5 = 5 + 5$

$4 + 6 = \underline{} + \underline{}$ $4 + \underline{} = 3 + \underline{}$

$2 + \underline{} = 3 + \underline{}$ $7 + \underline{} = 5 + \underline{}$

13

Grow and Shrink

For Grades K–2

CONTENT AREA

Number and Operations

MATERIALS

- ten-frames, 1 per student (see Blackline masters)
- interlocking cubes, such as Multilink, Snap, or Unifix cubes, 10 per student
- 2 dice, each numbered 0–5 (or use dice numbered 1–6 and substitute the 6 with 0)

TIME

ten minutes (fifteen minutes to introduce the activity on the first day)

Overview

Ten-frames are 2-by-5 arrays in which counters, cubes, or dots are placed to illustrate numbers. In this classroom activity, the teacher (or a student volunteer) rolls a pair of dice, each numbered 0–5. Students add to find the total number of dots and then show that quantity on their ten-frames using cubes. After each new roll, the children examine their ten-frames and change them to show the new total.

Ten-frames help children relate numbers to other numbers, especially to 5 and 10. For example, 7 is 3 away from 10, or 7 is 5 and 2 more. *Grow and Shrink* can help students learn about number relationships, provide counting practice, and serve as an informal context for exploring addition and subtraction.

Activity Directions

1. Distribute to each student one ten-frame and ten cubes.
2. Roll the dice or have a student volunteer roll them.
3. Record the roll on the board using two boxes to represent the dice and dots to represent the two numbers rolled. Have the students find the total rolled together.
4. Have the students use their ten-frames and cubes to show the total on the dice.
5. Continue rolling the dice. Record each roll on the board, have the students figure the total rolled, and then direct the students to place cubes on their ten-frames to match the sum shown on the two dice.

Key Questions

- How many dots is __ and __ more? How do you know?
- How many cubes should you put on your ten-frames? Explain.
- How many more cubes do we need to make ten?

From the Classroom

Frannie MacKenzie's students had been working with ten-frames for about a week or so when I introduced the math activity *Grow and Shrink*. As with the other ten-frame activities (see *Ten-Frames* on page 138 and *Ten-Frames Cleared* on page 142), I gathered the class on the rug area and gave each student a ten-frame and ten Snap Cubes.

After distributing the materials, I showed the class the pair of dice we would use for the game. On the faces of each die were dot arrangements from zero dots to five dots. I purposely used dice with dots so that the children could connect numbers to the quantities that they represented. In future games I planned to use dice with the numerals 0–5 on the faces.

I rolled the dice to begin the game. As I rolled, I told the students that we would add the dots together to find out how many cubes to place on our ten-frames. So that everyone could see the outcome, I drew two boxes on the board to represent the dice, one with two dots inside, and the other with one dot to show the first roll. On subsequent rolls, I changed the number of dots inside each box to match the outcome of the roll.

"How many dots is two and one more?" I asked.

"Three!" several students called out.

"Raise your hand if you want to come up and show and tell how you know," I said. I waited for several seconds before calling on a volunteer. Sometimes I have to literally count the seconds in my head (I usually count to fifteen or more) so that I provide sufficient think time for students. As I waited, more students raised their hands. I finally called on Victor. He walked up to the drawings of the dice on the board.

"One, two, and three," he said, first pointing to each dot on one die and then touching the dot on the other die.

"Is there another way to figure the total number of dots?" I asked.

"I just looked at them and knew there were three," Jill shared.

"I know that two plus one is three," Carlos said in a confident tone.

"I did two," Maureen said, pointing to the first die. "Then the other one makes three."

Jill just "saw" the total number of dots without counting. Maureen counted on from the larger quantity (two). And Carlos seemed to have internalized the number combination. Victor, on the other hand, still had to count every dot one by one. As a teacher, I'm constantly watching and waiting for students to make conceptual leaps like moving from counting from one to counting on. Although these leaps take time and experience, listening to others share their methods (including the teacher) can also help students develop their mathematical thinking.

Next I directed the students to show the total number of dots (three) on their ten-frames using cubes.

"How many cubes should you put on your ten-frames?" I asked.

"Three!" the students called out.

"And how many cubes should you put in each box?" I asked, checking to make sure they remembered from their earlier work with the ten-frames.

"One!" they responded.

As students placed their cubes, I quickly made a visual sweep of their ten-frames to check how they were doing. Once everyone was ready, I rolled the dice again and recorded on the board the second roll: four dots in one box and three dots in the other box. Next, I directed the students to find the total and asked for a couple of volunteers to explain their methods. Then I gave directions for the next step in the game.

"Now, because there are seven dots showing on the dice, change your ten-frame so that there are seven cubes on it, not three," I told the class.

I waited until each student had changed his or her ten-frame from three cubes to seven cubes.

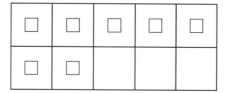

"Who can tell us how you figured out how to put seven cubes on your ten-frame?" I asked the class.

"I took all my cubes off and then counted one, two, three, all the way up to seven cubes," Tim explained.

"I kept my three cubes on and then added up to get to seven," Maureen said, demonstrating with the cubes how she counted on from three.

I then asked the following question to push their thinking. "How many more cubes do we need to make ten?"

This question stumped some of the students. Several counted on from seven to figure the answer, and one student counted back from ten.

We continued with this process of rolling the dice, finding the total, and changing the number of cubes on the ten-frames several more times before bringing the activity to a close.

While showing numbers on the ten-frames is good practice for many second graders, it is not so easy for kindergartners and first graders. After each roll, I watched to see how students decided to change their ten-frames. Did they clear off the entire frame and start over with each number? Did they just know what the number looked like? Did they count on or count back from the previous number of cubes? At one point during the activity, when students had to change their ten-frames from six cubes to three cubes, Amanda remarked, "This is like adding and take away!" This astute observation showed me that Amanda recognized, in her own way, that *Grow and Shrink* could serve as an informal context for exploring addition and subtraction.

"Yes," I replied to Amanda. "When we add cubes, the amount grows, and when we take away cubes, the total amount shrinks."

Extending the Activity

Use two ten-frames and up to four of the 0–5 dice.

14

Guess My Number

For Grades K-2

CONTENT AREA

Number and Operations

MATERIALS

- 2 sticky notes, 1 with a left-facing arrow and 1 with a right-facing arrow (grades K-1)

TIME

ten to fifteen minutes

Overview

In this activity, students guess a secret number from within a range of numbers. The teacher tells them whether the secret number is greater or less than their guesses, and they continue to refine their guesses based on that information. *Guess My Number* develops students' number sense by giving them opportunities to think about the relationships between and among numbers and by helping them gain an understanding of the relative position and magnitude of whole numbers.

Activity Directions

1. Choose a secret number.
2. Draw a number line on the board and tell the class the range of numbers your number falls within (1 to 10, 50 to 100, 1 to 100, whatever).
3. Have individual students guess your secret number; if the guess is incorrect, announce whether your number is greater or less than the number suggested. For grades K–1, use sticky notes with left- and right-facing arrows on them to help students see how their guesses continue to narrow the options for the secret number.
4. Continue until someone guesses your secret number.

Key Questions

- I'm thinking of a number between __ and __. What's your guess?
- What numbers are good guesses? Why?
- What do you know about my number?

From a Kindergarten Classroom

Kimberly Sharman's kindergartners filed in from recess and sat on the carpet at the front of the room. Her students were all English language learners; Spanish was their native language.

"Today we're going to play a guessing game," I began. "But before we play, we're going to warm up our brains and think about numbers." When I gave these directions, I was careful to speak slowly, enunciate each word clearly, and use gestures whenever possible. All of these techniques can help English language learners as they learn academic content in a second language.

To give the students practice identifying numbers and quantities, I held up five fingers and asked the class, "How many fingers am I holding up?"

"Five!" the students answered in unison. I then held up three fingers, then ten, and then two. Each time everyone seemed to instantly know how many fingers I was showing. Next, I held up seven fingers.

"Now how many?" I asked. This time, the students seemed a little hesitant. Many students said seven, some said six, and a few thought I was holding up eight fingers. Ana volunteered to come up and stand beside me to show and tell us what she thought.

"I think there are seven fingers," she said.

"How do you know there are seven?" I asked. Ana did not respond to my question. She just stood there, staring at my fingers.

"Ana, you can count them!" a boy on the rug suggested.

Ana took the boy's suggestion and counted my raised fingers. "One, two, three, four . . . ," she counted, all the way to seven.

Next, I drew a number line on the board. As I recorded the numbers *0–10*, I directed the students to count with me.

```
0   1   2   3   4   5   6   7   8   9   10
```

I then pointed to the number 4 and asked the students to tell me the name of that number and to show me the amount with their fingers. This allowed me to informally assess students' ability to identify numbers by their names and the quantities they represented. After the number 4, I continued pointing to a variety of numbers on the number line before introducing *Guess My Number*.

"OK, now that we've warmed up our brains, we're going to play a guessing game," I told the class. "I'm going to think of a number and you're going to try to guess what it is. Ready?"

I squinted my eyes and touched my index finger to my forehead, giving the impression that I was thinking of a number.

"I've got it now!" I said. "I'm thinking of a number that's on our number line. It could be zero, one, two, all the way up to ten. Raise your hand if you have a guess."

The students were very excited to guess. I waited several seconds to give them think time; then I called on David, who guessed ten. My secret number was eight, so I placed a sticky note with a left-facing arrow drawn on it under David's guess to give the class a clue:

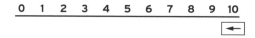

"My number is less than ten," I told the class, pointing to the arrow on the sticky note and gesturing to all the numbers below 10. "Who has another guess?"

Daniela guessed the number two, so I placed another sticky note, with a right-facing arrow drawn on it, underneath her guess:

"My number is between two and ten," I told the class. "It's less than ten and greater than two." I used my finger to sweep across the numbers between 2 and 10 and said, "My number is one of these numbers."

Adriana guessed six, so I moved the left sticky note from the 2 to the 6:

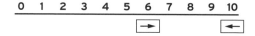

Now the students were very excited and I had to remind them to raise their hands to make a guess. Because it was so difficult for the students to contain themselves, I directed them to whisper their guesses to a neighbor. Then I took Martin's guess, which was nine. I moved the right sticky note from 10 and placed it underneath Martin's guess:

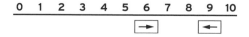

"Which numbers are good guesses now?" I asked. The students were eager to guess my secret number. They all seemed to know that they had narrowed it down to two possibilities: seven or eight. We ended the game when Victor correctly guessed my number.

From a Second-Grade Classroom

As Robin Gordon's second graders watched, I quickly drew a number line on the board like this:

```
0              x                    50
```

"I'm thinking of a number and my number is where the X is on this number line," I told the class. "Is my number less or greater than fifty?"

"Less!" answered the students. This seemed pretty obvious to them. I then asked, "Is my number less or greater than ten?"

"It's closer to ten, because ten is close to zero and far away from fifty," River observed.

Next, I wrote the number *10* on the number line:

```
0      10     x                    50
```

"Now that you know where ten is on the number line, talk with a partner and try to guess my number," I told the class. As partners discussed, I quickly circulated, listening to students and making sure that everyone was focused. Then I asked for the group's attention and called on Tanisha.

"I think your number is fifteen, 'cause it's close to ten."

"I think it's bigger than fifteen, maybe sixteen or seventeen," Carlos said.

"Where would twenty-five go?" I asked the class.

"It's right in the middle of the number line, 'cause twenty-five plus twenty-five is fifty," Beta explained.

"Does everyone agree with Beta? Does that make sense?" I asked. Students nodded their agreement and I wrote the number *25* between the 0 and the 50 on the number line:

```
0      10   x   25              50
```

"Now what do you know about my number?" I asked.

"It's between ten and twenty-five," Tana said.

"In a whisper voice, tell me what you think my number is," I directed. I listened carefully to students' guesses to check for reasonableness. The guesses I heard ranged from fourteen to twenty. Finally, I revealed my secret number to the class, which was nineteen.

Extending the Activity

- Use a 1–100 chart rather than a number line.
- Give an initial clue before beginning the guessing game. Possible clues:

> The number is an odd number.
> The number is an even number.
> The digit in the tens place is greater than the digit in the ones place.
> The digit in the ones place is greater than the digit in the tens place.
> You can land on the number by counting by twos, fives, or tens.
> The number ends with a zero.

Heavier or Lighter?

For Grades K-2

15

Overview

In the primary grades, children are expected to recognize attributes of weight and use appropriate tools to order and compare objects according to these attributes.

There is a difference between measuring an object's weight and measuring its mass. Weight is a measure of the pull or force of gravity on an object; it is measured using a spring scale. Mass is the amount of matter in an object and a measure of the force needed to accelerate it; mass is measured using a balance. In the primary grades, making the distinction between an object's weight and mass isn't necessary. However, since a balance is used to compare objects in this activity, there is no reference to weight. Rather, students are asked to find out which object is *heavier* and which is *lighter*.

Activity Directions

1. Show students a balance and ask them what they think it is used for.
2. Ask students to think of and discuss different things they can measure.
3. Introduce the words *heavier* and *lighter*. Tell students that we can use a balance to measure whether one object is heavier or lighter than another object.
4. Show the students two classroom objects and have them predict which is heavier and which is lighter.
5. Ask a volunteer to hold two classroom objects in his or her hands (one object in one hand and another object in the other hand). Ask the student which is heavier and which is lighter.
6. To check which object is heavier, have the volunteer place one object on one side of the balance and the other object on the other side of the balance.
7. Repeat Steps 4–6 using other classroom objects.

CONTENT AREA

Measurement

MATERIALS

- balance scale or pan balance
- assorted classroom items (e.g., scissors, pencil, marker, eraser, calculator, book, etc.)

TIME

fifteen minutes

Key Questions

- Show students a balance and ask them what it is and what they think it is used for.
- What are some different things we can measure?
- Which object do you think is heavier, _____ or _____? Explain.
- How will we know which object is heavier or lighter?

From the Classroom

Elisabeth Frausto showed her students a red plastic balance that she had used with them earlier in the year to compare pumpkins to see which ones were heavier and which were lighter.

"Does anyone remember what this is?" she asked, pointing to the balance.

"We put the pumpkins on it and we saw which side went down more," Roger recalled.

"That's right," Elisabeth acknowledged. "Today, we're going to explore the idea of measurement again with the balance."

As she always does when introducing or revisiting a math topic or concept, Elisabeth tapped her students' prior knowledge about measurement.

"What are some different things we can measure?" she asked.

"Like how tall I am," Elianna said.

"We can get cubes to see if my arm is bigger than my leg," Zuriel chimed in.

"Yes, we can measure how long something is or how tall it is," Elisabeth said. "We can also use the balance to measure how heavy something is or how light it is compared with other things." She wrote the words *heavier* and *lighter* on a piece of chart paper and had the students read the words aloud. She then gathered her students on the rug in a circle, with the balance and a box of classroom objects in the middle for students to see.

From the box, Elisabeth picked up a Unifix cube and held it in one hand. Next, she picked up a beanbag from the box and held it in her other hand. She moved her hands up and down and asked the students which they thought was heavier, the cube or the beanbag. Most of the students thought the beanbag was heavier.

"What makes you think the beanbag is heavier?" she asked the class.

"Because the beanbag is more bigger," Justin said. The students nodded their heads in agreement. It is common for young children to think that if an object is big, it will be heavy.

"I'm going to place the beanbag on one side of the balance and the Unifix cube on the other side," Elisabeth told the class. "How will we know which one is heavier?"

"It will go down more," Katie said. The other students seemed to agree. To check, Elisabeth placed the cube and the beanbag on either side of the balance; the students were correct: the beanbag touched the floor. The students cheered.

"Which is heavier?" Elisabeth asked the class.

"The beanbag!" the students exclaimed.

To assist the students with using the new vocabulary, Elisabeth wrote these two sentence frames on the board:

The _____ is heavier than the _____.
The _____ is lighter than the _____.

Using the sentence frames for support, Elisabeth had her students compare the objects.

"The beanbag is heavier than the cube," the students read as Elisabeth pointed to the words in the sentence frame. They continued, "The cube is lighter than the beanbag."

Next, Elisabeth asked for a volunteer to come up and hold a 1-inch plastic bear in one hand and a 3-inch plush bear in the other hand. Sophie willingly volunteered.

"Which do you think is heavier?" Elisabeth asked Sophie.

Sophie held the two objects, one in each hand, and moved them up and down, trying to sense which object was heavier. After a few seconds, she guessed that the plush bear was heavier. The students in the class nodded their agreement.

To check, Sophie and Elisabeth placed the objects on the balance, and the plastic bear fell lower than the plush bear. Several students gasped; it was clear that the class was surprised at the result.

"So what are you thinking right now?" Elisabeth asked. She waited several seconds to give the students some time to think, and then she called on Serena.

"You have to put it on there to know if it's heavier!" Serena exclaimed, pointing to the balance.

"Just 'cause it looks heavier doesn't mean it is," Richard added.

"It might be bigger, but if it's bigger it might not be heavier," Justin reasoned.

Before moving on to the next two objects, Elisabeth had her students compare the plastic bear and the plush bear using the sentence frames.

"The plastic bear is heavier than the plush bear," the students recited in a choral voice.

"The plush bear is lighter than the plastic bear," they continued, with Elisabeth's direction.

Next, Elisabeth asked Richard to come to the front of the rug and hold a marker in one hand and a glue stick in the other.

"Which do you think is heavier?" Elisabeth asked him.

Richard thought that the glue stick was heavier, but the students in the class had mixed opinions.

To test, Elisabeth asked Richard to place the objects on either side of the balance. The glue stick went lower.

"Which is lighter?" Elisabeth asked.

"The marker!" students responded.

"How can we tell that the marker is lighter than the glue stick?" Elisabeth asked.

"It's more up," Donavyn said. "The side that the glue stick is on is down and the side that the marker is on is up."

Before moving on, Elisabeth had her students use the sentence frames to compare the marker and the glue stick. Then she asked the students to compare a few more classroom objects, each time eliciting predictions and then asking a volunteer to check by using his or her hands and then using the balance.

Extending the Activity

- Have students compare three classroom objects.
- Have students predict some objects that are heavier or lighter than a certain object. Then have them check their predictions using their hands and then the balance.

How Long? How Tall?

For Grades K-2

Overview

Students in the primary grades are expected to "recognize the attributes of length, compare objects according to this attribute, and understand how to measure using nonstandard and standard units" (NCTM 2000, 102). In this activity, students learn about length and height as measurable attributes. Students compare the length or height of different objects in the room with a train of twenty cubes. Then they use the cube train to measure the object.

Activity Directions

1. Ask students what it means to measure something or what they already know about measuring.
2. Show the class a train of twenty interlocking cubes. With the class, count the number of cubes in the train.
3. Choose an object in the room (or have a student choose an object) and ask the students to estimate whether the object's length is longer or shorter than the length of the cube train. Elicit students' ideas.
4. Call on a volunteer to help you compare the object with the cube train.
5. Measure the object using the cube train.
6. Repeat Steps 3–5, using a different object (and a different dimension of the object, such as width) in the room.

Key Questions

- What does it mean to measure something?
- What do you know about measurement?
- Do you think __ is longer or shorter than the cube train?
- Do you think __ is taller or shorter than the cube train?

CONTENT AREA

Measurement

MATERIALS

- 20 interlocking cubes, such as Multilink, Snap, or Unifix cubes, snapped into a train

TIME

ten minutes (fifteen minutes to introduce the activity on the first day)

From the Classroom

"What does it mean to measure something?" I asked Elisabeth Frausto's students. I wrote the word *measure* on the class math vocabulary chart.

"What do you know about measurement?" I asked again, using a slightly broader question. I wanted to tap students' prior knowledge about measurement before we actually started measuring. I was curious to hear what they already knew.

"It means count to see how long something is," Justin said.

"When you measure, you use a measuring tape," Angie added.

"And you can also use a ruler," Donavyn chimed in.

"Anything else that you know about measuring?" I probed.

"You measure to find out how long something is," Gabriella said.

"Or to measure how wide or how heavy something is," Miles said. "Like I can find out how much I weigh."

After listening to a few students' ideas about measurement, I held up a train of twenty Snap Cubes.

"Let's see how *long* this cube train is," I told the class as I wrote the word *long* on the vocabulary chart. "We're going to use it to measure things."

The students counted the cube train with me as I touched each Snap Cube, modeling a one-to-one correspondence between the object touched and the count. When we finished counting twenty Snap Cubes, I told the class what we were going to do.

"Today we're going to use this Snap Cube train and compare it with things in the room," I began. I then told the students to look at their little finger and think about whether it was longer or shorter than the cube train. As students were looking at their fingers and thinking, I wrote the words *longer* and *shorter* on the class chart.

"Shorter!" the students chorused. They all seemed convinced that their little finger was shorter than the cube train.

I called on Emme to come up front and compare her little finger with the cube train. It was indeed a lot shorter than the cube train. The students seemed delighted with their estimates. The students counted with me as we measured the length of Emme's little finger, which measured three cubes.

Next, I asked the students to compare their height with the cube train. I recorded the words *height* and *taller* on the chart.

"Do you think you are taller or shorter than the cube train?" I asked. "When we measure our length standing up, we usually say *taller* rather than *longer*. We are measuring our *height*."

Everyone seemed to think he or she was taller than the cube train. I called Serena to come up to the front of the class. I held the cube train next to her as she stood up straight. Serena was a lot taller than the cube train. In fact, I carefully showed the students that two and a half of the cube trains equaled Serena's height.

"How many cubes tall do you think Serena is?" I asked. I gave the students some time to think. After several seconds, only Tobias had his hand up.

"She's fifty cubes tall!" he exclaimed. "Twenty and twenty is forty, and I added ten more to that," he explained.

As we confirmed Tobias's idea, I thought about his math ability compared with that of the rest of the students in the class. Although mentally determining Serena's height in cubes seemed inaccessible to most of the students, it's important to pose questions that challenge the range of student abilities.

"Let's compare your foot with the cube train," I then said to the class. "Do you think your foot is longer or shorter than the cube train?"

Most students thought their foot would be shorter. To check, I asked Kiara to come up front and place her foot on a chair so that I could compare the length of the cube train with the length of her foot. As I held the cube train next to Kiara's foot, I explained that one end of the cube train must line up with one end of the thing that we were measuring. In this case, it was Kiara's foot.

After we measured how many cubes long Kiara's foot was, I held up a book from the classroom library.

"Let's estimate whether the cube train will be longer than this book," I said.

I showed the class the width of the book compared with its length to point out the attribute of the book that we were comparing with the cube train.

"Do you think the cube train is *longer* or *shorter* than the book?" I asked, emphasizing the measurement words. As with the other objects, I elicited students' estimates and then directly compared the book with the cube train. Finally, we measured the length of the book using the cube train.

We continued comparing objects in the room with the Snap Cube train: the length of a pencil, the length of a class poster, and the length of one of the tables in the class.

To finish the activity, I pointed to the measurement words I'd written on the chart and read them aloud as the class read along with me: *measure, height, long, longer, shorter, taller*.

Extending the Activity

- Compare and measure other items in the classroom.
- Use a longer or shorter cube train when comparing and then measuring objects.
- Use standard measurement units to compare and then measure with a ruler, a yardstick, a meter stick, and a measuring tape.
- Give each student a cube train of his or her own to compare, measure, and record the measurements of objects. Students can work in pairs for this activity.

In One Minute

For Grades K-2

CONTENT AREA

Measurement

MATERIALS

- analog clock with a second hand (on the classroom wall) or a watch with a second hand
- plastic or cardboard analog clock with movable hour and minute hands

TIME

fifteen minutes

Overview

For young children, learning to tell time on an analog clock requires ongoing practice. In addition to learning how to read a clock, students need to learn about seconds, minutes, and hours and develop some concept of how long these units are.

In this activity, students first practice telling time to the hour and half hour on an analog clock. Then students develop their sense of one minute when they see how many times they can perform an activity (write letters, write their name, build a tower with cubes, draw stars, etc.) in one minute.

Activity Directions

1. Show students a plastic or cardboard analog clock and ask them what they notice about the clock and what they know.
2. Move the hands to several different hour and half-hour positions and have students identify the time.
3. On the board, write important activities that happen during the day and ask the students at what times they occur. Draw clock faces next to the times and call on volunteers to draw in the hour and minute hands to show the times for each activity.
4. Direct students' attention to the second hand on the wall clock (or a watch). While you time one minute, have students close their eyes and raise their hands when they think one minute has passed.
5. Ask students to estimate how many letters of the alphabet you can write on the board in one minute. Then have them time you as you write the letters of the alphabet. Together with the class, count the letters first by ones and then by twos to find the total amount.
6. Direct students to write as many letters of the alphabet as they can in one minute as you time them. When they are finished, have them count their letters by ones and twos to find the total amount.

Key Questions

- What do you notice and know about the clock?
- What time is it on the clock?
- What time of day does _____ occur?
- How many seconds are there in one minute?
- About how many letters do you think I can write in one minute?
- If we count the letters by twos, will there still be _____? Explain.

From the Classroom

Although Sharon Fargason's students had been taught how to tell time earlier in the year, they hadn't had practice doing so for quite a while. Curious to see what they still remembered, I held up a plastic analog clock and asked the students to turn to a partner and talk about everything they knew about the clock. After a minute or so, I called for the students' attention.

The students seemed to know quite a bit. They knew about the hour hand and the minute hand. Richard noted that there are sixty minutes in an hour, and Nith commented that there are five minutes between each number on the clock. Jessica said that there are numbers on the clock, starting at 12 and going all the way back to 12 again.

After students had finished sharing what they knew and noticed about the clock, I rotated the hour hand and minute hand on the plastic clock so that it read one o'clock. I directed the students to call out the correct time in unison so that everyone would get practice. I continued to move the hands to different locations, providing students with experience in telling time to the hour and to the half hour. Each time, I directed the class to call out the correct time in a choral voice.

Next, I wrote important activities on the board that happened during the day. I asked the students if anyone knew at what time the activities occurred. If someone knew the correct answer, I wrote in the time; if no one knew, I provided the correct answer. Next to each activity, I quickly drew a clock face and asked for volunteers to come up and draw where the hands belonged.

School starts   8:00

Lunch   12:00

Recess   10:30

Dismissal   2:30

After we practiced reading the times for each activity during the day, I directed the students' attention to the red second hand that was moving around the clock on the wall. I told them that the red hand was the second hand and measured time in seconds. When I asked the class how many seconds there are in one minute, only Jose knew that there were sixty.

"I want you to get a sense of how long sixty seconds, or one minute, is," I told the class. "When I say 'go,' I want you all to close your eyes and raise your hand when you think one minute has passed. I'll keep track and watch the second hand on the clock and tell you when one minute is up."

"Can we count to sixty when our eyes are closed?" Tracy asked, revealing that she remembered how many seconds there are in one minute.

"Sure," I responded.

There was much excitement in the room as I called out, "Ready, set, go!"

As the seconds ticked off on the wall clock, students raised their hands at different times. Some hands shot up after only ten seconds, while other students came closer to accurately judging the length of time that had passed. When I told them to open their eyes, many students commented on how long a minute seemed to them. When we were finished, I asked the class a question.

"About how many letters of the alphabet do you think I can write on the board in one minute?"

I elicited ideas from the students, and their estimates ranged from "about four" to "about twenty-seven."

I then directed the class to watch the second hand on the clock and time me as I wrote the letters of the alphabet on the board. I reminded them that if I got to the letter Z, I would begin again, writing the letter A, then B, and so forth until one minute had passed.

All students' eyes were glued to the clock as they kept track of the second hand. When one minute was up, they all shouted, "Stop!" I had written quite a few letters on the board and the students were surprised. Together, we counted the letters by ones and I recorded the total of *50* on the board.

"If we count the letters by twos, will there still be fifty?" I asked.

While most of Sharon's first graders thought that no matter how we counted the letters, the amount would stay the same, this idea is not obvious to all young children. To check, we counted by twos as I circled pairs of letters.

Next, I instructed the students on what they were to do at their seats. "Get a piece of paper and a pencil and write your name on your paper. Wait until I say 'go!' before writing letters. When I say 'stop,' count your letters by ones and record how many letters you wrote. Then count again by twos."

When one minute had passed, I signaled the students to stop. Then I circulated through the room to check how accurate they were with their counts and to offer help if needed as students counted by twos. Figures 17–1 and 17–2 show two students' alphabet papers.

Figure 17-1 Deanna wrote fifty letters of the alphabet in one minute.

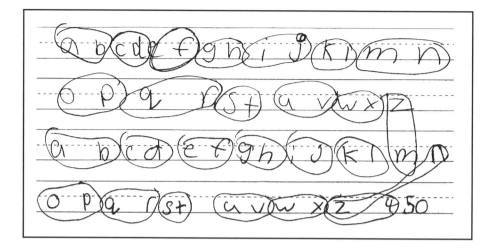

Figure 17-2 Justin counted his letters by twos and got twenty-four.

Extending the Activity

Other activities for students to do in one minute:

> write numbers
> write their first name
> write their last name
> build towers using interlocking cubes
> draw stars

Measuring Area

For Grades K-2

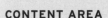

Overview

In the primary grades, students are expected to "recognize the measurable attributes of objects, understand how to measure using nonstandard and standard units, and develop common referents or benchmarks for measures to make comparisons and estimates" (NCTM 2000, 102). In this activity, students learn about area as a measurable attribute. Using 1-inch square color tiles, students estimate and then measure the area of a piece of paper.

Activity Directions

1. Show students a piece of paper that measures 8 inches by 3 inches. To introduce the words *perimeter* and *area* to students, point first to the paper's perimeter and explain to the students that the perimeter is the outside edge that goes around the piece of paper. Then point to the area and explain that the paper's area is the space inside the perimeter.
2. Provide a referent or benchmark for estimating the area of the paper by placing ten color tiles of one color in the area of the paper.
3. Together with the students, count the ten tiles, touching each tile as you count.
4. Ask students to estimate how many tiles will fill the area of the piece of paper, based on what they have discovered so far.
5. Place ten more tiles of a different color in the area of the piece of paper.
6. Ask the students how many tiles they think are on the paper, and then count the tiles together, first by ones and then by tens.
7. Now that they have a benchmark of twenty tiles, ask students to reestimate how many tiles will fill the area of the paper.

CONTENT AREA

Measurement

MATERIALS

- color tiles, at least 40 with some combination of the four colors
- white copier paper of varying shapes and sizes

TIME

ten to fifteen minutes

8. Completely fill in the area of the paper using a third color, then count the tiles together with the students, first by ones and then by tens.

Key Questions

- How many tiles will fit in the *area* of the piece of paper?
- Here are ten tiles. How many tiles do you think will cover all of the paper?

From the Classroom

Elisabeth Frausto's students were sitting in their "circle spots" around the edge of the rug, ready to begin the lesson.

"I see that everyone is ready, sitting on the *perimeter*, or edge, of the rug," I said to the class. I like to use correct math terms along with every-day words to help build students' vocabulary comprehension.

I continued, "I notice that the rug's *area*, or the space inside, is empty." I gestured with my hand at the rug's area as I spoke.

Next, I placed an 8-by-3-inch piece of white copier paper on the rug in clear view of the students. The piece of paper's area measured 24 inches, using 1-inch square color tiles as units of measure. I chose this size paper for the activity because twenty-four seemed like an appropriate number for kindergartners to estimate and count. You can vary the size and shape of the paper to challenge students at different grade levels or at different ability levels.

"Just like the rug we're sitting on, this piece of paper has an outside edge, or *perimeter*," I told the class. I directed the students to say the word *perimeter* aloud as I traced the paper's perimeter with my index finger.

"And like the rug, this piece of paper has a space inside the perimeter called the *area*," I explained, emphasizing the new math vocabulary word. Again, I had the class say the word *area* aloud as I pointed to the paper's area using the palm of my hand. I then wrote the words *area* and *perimeter* on the board. Although this activity focuses on measuring area, I also wanted to raise students' awareness of perimeter, another important measurable attribute of objects.

With the students watching attentively, I carefully placed ten green color tiles on the piece of paper and directed the students to count the tiles with me. As we counted aloud together, I touched each tile, one by one, to model one-to-one correspondence.

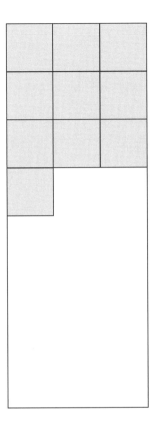

"This is what ten tiles looks like on the paper," I said to the class. Showing students what ten tiles looks like provides them with a referent, or benchmark, from which to make estimates.

Pointing to the area of the piece of paper with the palm of my hand, I said, "I want you each to think about how many tiles will fit in the *area* of the piece of paper."

After giving the students some individual think time, I elicited estimates. I wasn't surprised to hear a range of ideas.

"I think about twenty," Areysi guessed.

"Sixty-four," Maria said.

"Maybe a hundred," Zuriel chimed in.

"I think about twenty-five tiles will cover the paper," John added.

Saul, who had very fragile number sense, guessed that one tile would fill the area of the piece of paper. I wasn't sure whether Saul understood my question, so I rephrased it for him.

"Here are ten green tiles," I began, pointing at the tiles on the paper. "How many tiles do you think it will take to cover all of the paper?"

Saul just sat, staring at me. I decided to offer a little support.

"There are ten already on the paper, Saul," I said. "Give us a number that's bigger than ten."

Saul thought for a moment, and then responded with the number fifteen.

"Yes, that's bigger than ten," I said in a reassuring tone of voice.

Next, I added ten yellow color tiles, placing them next to the ten green tiles that were already on the paper.

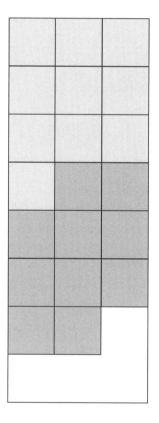

"How many tiles are on the paper now?" I asked.

"There's twenty!" Areysi exclaimed. "'Cause ten greens and ten yellows make twenty!"

I was surprised that Areysi knew the answer so quickly. Five- and six-year-olds typically count one by one rather than count groups of objects. Had Areysi not come up with the idea of counting tens, I would have introduced the idea.

"Let's check to see if Areysi is correct," I said.

The students counted along with me as I pointed to each of the twenty tiles. Then I had the class count the tiles by tens. I motioned to the group of green tiles first as we said, "Ten!" in a choral voice, then I pointed to the group of ten yellow tiles as we said, "Twenty!"

"So there are twenty tiles on the paper now," I then said. "Now how many tiles do you think will cover the area of the paper? Talk to your partner about your new estimate."

After the room quieted, I asked the question again and elicited some estimates.

"I still think twenty-five," John said. "There's twenty and room for a little bit more."

"Thirty!" Roger boomed.

"Other ideas?" I whispered, signaling to students that quiet voices were preferred.

"I think maybe twenty-three," Donavyn said.

"A little more than twenty," Sophie offered.

I was happy to hear that students' estimates were more refined than before and that students seemed comfortable with changing their estimates as they got more information.

To complete the activity, I finished covering the area of the paper with red tiles.

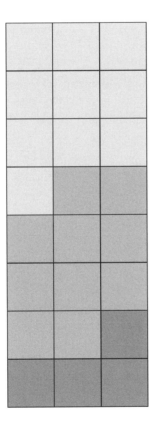

Together, we counted the twenty-four tiles by ones. Then we counted them by tens—first we counted the ten green tiles, then the ten yellow ones, and finally we counted on from twenty to twenty-four using the red tiles. On the board, I recorded this sentence:

The paper's area measures 24 tiles.

As I pointed to each word, I directed the students to read aloud the sentence with me. Finally, I recorded the area of the piece of paper to begin a classroom chart.

Extending the Activity

- Use pieces of paper of different shapes and sizes (e.g., 5 inches by 5 inches; 10 inches by 5 inches; 10 inches by 10 inches; and so on). Record the area of each piece of paper and post it in the classroom.
- Give each student his or her own piece of paper and have the students estimate and then figure the area using color tiles, cubes, or other nonstandard units of measure.
- Give students a different-sized paper and ask them to estimate if its area is greater than, less than, or equivalent to the first paper. Have them figure the area of the new piece of paper using color tiles to check their estimates.
- Have students trace their mitt print or footprint and figure the area using color tiles, cubes, or other nonstandard units of measure.

More or Less? Version 1

For Grades K–2

19

Overview

The concepts of *more*, *less*, and *same* are basic relationships contributing to the overall concept of number. In this activity, students gain experience with these concepts. Students are also asked to think about part-part-whole relationships. For example, students see that when twenty two-color counters are tossed, a variety of combinations of yellow and red can result: ten red and ten yellow, nine red and eleven yellow, and so on.

Activity Directions

1. Put twenty two-color counters in a cup. (For kindergartners, start with ten counters and then fifteen before using twenty.)
2. Shake the cup and spill the counters onto the rug in a pile so all students can see them.
3. Ask the students whether there are more red, more yellow, or about the same amount of each color. Elicit students' ideas.
4. Sort the counters into two separate groups by color: one red group and one yellow group.
5. Again ask the students whether there are more red, more yellow, or about the same amount of each color. Elicit students' ideas.
6. To help the students compare the number of red counters with the number of yellow counters, place the counters in two lines on the rug so that there is a red and a yellow next to each other, matched one to one.
7. Once more, ask students whether there are more red, more yellow, or about the same amount of each color. Elicit students' ideas.
8. With the students, count the total number of yellow counters. Then ask how many red counters there are and how many counters altogether.

CONTENT AREA

Number and Operations

MATERIALS

- 20 two-color counters
- 1 cup

TIME

ten minutes (fifteen minutes to introduce the activity on the first day)

Key Questions

- Are there more red counters, more yellow counters, or about the same amount of each color?
- How can we find out whether there are more red counters or more yellow counters?
- How many red counters and yellow counters are there altogether?

From the Classroom

Elisabeth Frausto held up a paper cup, showing it to her students, who were assembled in a circle on the rug. Inside the cup were twenty counters; one side of each counter was red and the other side was yellow.

"There are twenty counters inside the cup today," Elisabeth began. She held up one of the counters, showing both sides. The class had experienced this activity for several months, first working with ten counters in the cup, then fifteen, and now twenty counters.

"I'm going to spill the counters onto the rug. I want you to think about whether there are more yellows, more reds, or about the same amount of reds and yellows."

As Elisabeth shook the cup, the students wiggled with excitement.

"Are you ready?" Elisabeth asked. "Show me you're ready." She waited until the students seemed calm and were sitting flat on the rug with their hands folded. She then spilled the counters onto the rug:

"Are there more red counters, more yellow counters, or about the same amount of each color?" Elisabeth asked.

The students in the circle offered a mix of opinions; some thought there were more yellow, some thought there were more red, and a few thought there were about the same amount of each color.

After eliciting students' ideas, Elisabeth sorted the reds and yellows into two groups, being careful not to flip any counters. She once again asked the students whether they thought there were more yellow or more red counters. This time, a majority of students thought there were more red counters.

"How can we find out whether there are more red counters or more yellow counters?" Elisabeth asked the class.

"Count them!" several students chorused.

"And match them up, one to one!" others advised.

The students knew that Elisabeth would match up the counters one to one because they'd seen her do it previously as part of the activity.

She then picked up one counter at a time and positioned a red next to a yellow until there were no more yellow counters left, leaving two extra red counters.

"Are there more reds or yellows?" Elisabeth asked the class.

"More reds!" several students chorused.

"There are less yellows!" other students chimed in.

Together with the students, Elisabeth counted the number of yellow counters. Once it was confirmed that there were nine yellows, Elisabeth asked the class how many red counters there were.

"There's eleven reds," Miles said.

"How did you figure it out?" Elisabeth asked.

"'Cause there are two more red than yellow. There are nine yellow and two more red than that, so that's eleven."

"So how many red counters and yellow counters altogether?" Elisabeth asked.

There were a few confused looks, but most students responded that there were twenty counters in all.

"There's twenty 'cause we started with twenty!" Sophie exclaimed.

Even though students had had previous experience with this activity using ten and fifteen counters, Elisabeth knew that some students would need more experience with the activity to realize that the total amount stays the same each time.

"How many reds are there?" Elisabeth asked again.

"Eleven!" students chorused.

"And how many yellows?"

"Nine!"

"What's eleven and nine more?" Elisabeth pressed.

"Twenty!" the class called back.

To finish the activity, Elisabeth recorded the equation on the board that represented the combination of twenty counters: $11 + 9 = 20$. She then repeated the activity one more time, putting the twenty counters back into the cup, shaking it, and spilling the counters onto the rug. This time, there were seven reds and thirteen yellows, a different number combination of twenty for students to work with.

Extending the Activity

- Use a different number of two-color counters (if you started with ten or fifteen, use twenty or twenty-five counters; if you started with twenty, use ten, fifteen, or twenty-five counters).
- Have students partner up, giving each pair a cup and twenty two-color counters. This way, students gain direct experience with the activity. Have students record the outcome of each spill by drawing a picture of the counters or writing an equation.

More or Less? Version 2

For Grade 2

20

Overview

In this activity, students are asked to estimate whether a sum, difference, or product is more or less than a target number. For example, students determine whether the sum of 25 + 25 will be more or less than 40, the target number.

Activity Directions

1. Determine a target number between twenty and one hundred, for example, forty.
2. Write the following question on the board: *Is the answer more than 40 or less than 40?*
3. Write an expression on the board. For example: 25 + 25 =.
4. Ask students whether they think the answer is more or less than forty (the target number) and elicit students' ideas.
5. Using the same target number, write a different expression on the board and repeat Step 4.

Key Question

- Is the answer more or less than the target number? How do you know?

From the Classroom

Frannie MacKenzie's second graders listened attentively as I introduced the day's activity.

CONTENT AREA

Number and Operations

MATERIALS

TIME

ten minutes (fifteen minutes to introduce the activity on the first day)

"I want you to silently read the question I write on the board, and then we'll read it aloud together," I began. I wrote the following question on the board:

Is the answer more than 40 or less than 40?

After we read the sentence aloud together, I wrote the following expression on the board:

25 + 25 =

"Think about whether the answer to twenty-five plus twenty-five is more or less than forty," I said. After several seconds of think time, I called on Paul.

"I think it's more than forty," he said. "'Cause twenty and twenty make forty and you have some fives to add onto that."

Frannie's students were accustomed to explaining their ideas. If Paul hadn't explained his thinking, I would have asked him to do so.

"Did anyone think of it in a different way?" I asked.

"I just know that twenty-five plus twenty-five is fifty, because twenty-five cents and twenty-five cents is fifty cents," Terry explained.

"Thinking about money helps, doesn't it?" I commented. "Ready for the next problem?" The students sat quietly, eager to find out what was coming. On the board, I wrote:

15 + 11 =

"See if you can figure out if the answer is more or less than forty without solving the whole problem," I said. "In the last problem, twenty-five plus twenty-five, Paul looked at the digits in the tens place to give him a clue."

I wanted students to begin to look at numbers from left to right, taking notice of the largest place values first. Often, students are encouraged by their teachers to start in the ones place when solving problems. However, when students look at the digits in the tens place first, it can give them a clue about number size.

"I think it's going to be less than forty," Manuel said. "There's a ten in fifteen and a ten in eleven, so that's twenty. Then you only have six more to add onto that."

Manuel seemed to have an understanding of the value of the digits in a number; this signals an understanding of place value.

After confirming Manuel's idea, I wrote the following expression on the board:

$20 + 35 =$

"What do you think?" I asked the class. "Is the answer more or less than forty?"

After giving the students a few seconds of think time, I called on Roberta.

"I know that twenty and twenty is forty, so twenty and thirty-five has to be more than forty," she explained.

So far, the students seemed to be using their number sense to think about the problems. I decided to try to challenge them by switching operations. On the board, I wrote:

$40 - 16 =$

"Turn to your partner and talk about whether you think the answer is going to be more or less than forty," I directed. As partners shared, I listened in on several conversations. Initially, many students thought the answer would be more than forty. But soon, students became aware of the operation sign and changed their minds.

"I think the answer will be less than forty, 'cause when you subtract, you take things away from forty, so it's getting smaller," Taylor explained. Other students nodded in agreement.

"OK, now I'm going to try to challenge you!" I said. I wrote the following expression on the board:

$40 \times 2 =$

"Who would like to read the expression to us?" I asked. "Alicia?"

"Forty times two equals . . . ," she said.

As before, I gave students time to think and talk to a partner before sharing with the class. When students were ready, I called on Graham.

"When you times a number by two, you double it," he said. "I read about that!"

I was impressed with his thinking because the students hadn't had much exposure to multiplication yet.

"That's right," I responded. "Forty times two is the same as forty plus forty. How much is that?"

"Eighty!" several students exclaimed.

"So forty times two is more than forty," I confirmed.

This ended the activity for the day. On subsequent days, Frannie changed the target number.

Extending the Activity

- Ask students to come up with different number sentences equal to the target number.
- Use different target numbers.

Number Strings

For Grades 1-2

Overview

In this math activity, students practice combining numbers in different ways using number strings. A number string is an expression, written in a horizontal format, that includes more than two addends. Number strings can be practiced after students have had experience combining two numbers.

Children in the primary grades often begin combining numbers using counting strategies. It is common for young children to approach a problem such as 7 + 6 by counting from one using counters or their fingers to show a group of seven and a group of six:

1, 2, 3, 4, 5, 6, 7   8, 9, 10, . . . 13

Other children might count on from six or seven:

They will say, "Six" and then count: 7, 8, 9, 10, 11, 12, 13
Or they will say, "Seven" and then count: 8, 9, 10, 11, 12, 13

With time and experience, students begin to use their understanding of number relations to solve problems. For example, to solve 7 + 6, a student might use her knowledge of doubles: "I know that six plus six is twelve, so one more makes thirteen" or "seven plus seven is fourteen and one less is thirteen."

Learning to solve problems by counting on or using number relations takes time and experience. Giving students practice on a regular basis with combining a string of numbers (e.g., 8 + 3 + 2) can help them learn efficient strategies for solving problems.

Activity Directions

1. Record a number string on the board for students to solve (e.g., 1 + 5 + 1 + 5).
2. Allow a minute or so for students to solve the problem.

CONTENT AREA

Number and Operations

MATERIALS

- interlocking cubes, such as Multilink, Snap, or Unifix cubes, 50 per pair of students
- optional: overhead projector

TIME

ten minutes

3. Elicit answers and strategies from a few volunteers and represent students' strategies on the board.
4. Using a new number string, repeat Steps 1–3, this time asking students to share their strategies with a partner before you lead a class discussion.

Key Questions

- What strategy did you use?
- Can you find any familiar number combinations?
- Can you find any combinations that make ten in the number string?
- Can you find any doubles in the number string?

From the Classroom

To begin the activity, I wrote this number string on the board:

1 + 5 + 1 + 5 =

The students in Shawn Yoshimoto's class were huddled close to me on the rug in the front of the room. They listened attentively as I gave them directions.

"I want you to solve this number string in your head," I directed. "When you have your answer, put your thumb up so I know you are finished."

I scanned the rug area, watching the children. Some were counting on their fingers in a hurried fashion. Several immediately put their thumbs in the air. A few took a while before they were ready. I know that providing sufficient wait time is important in math class. It gives students time to formulate their thoughts. This is especially true for English language learners, who are learning mathematics *and* learning a new language at the same time.

After about a minute or so, I asked the students to raise their hands if they wanted to share their answers and tell how they solved the problem. I told the students that when someone tells *how* he solved a problem, he is telling about his *strategy*. I quickly wrote the word *strategy* on the board.

Rosa explained, "It's twelve. I counted."

"How did you count?" I asked. "What number did you start with?"

"I started with one," Rosa replied, almost in a whisper. "Then I went two, three, four, five, six."

"So you started with one and you counted on five more to get six?" I said, paraphrasing Rosa's words for the benefit of the rest of the class. "Then what did you do?"

She continued, "Then I added the one, and that's seven, and then I counted on five more."

"Tell us or show us how you did that," I said. "You had seven and you counted on five. Show and tell us what you did next."

"Seven," she began. Rosa then held up five fingers for the class to see. She then counted on, "Eight, nine, ten, eleven, twelve."

Sometimes getting students to articulate their strategies is an arduous task that takes lots of questioning, prompting, paraphrasing, and encouragement. And it isn't always easy to keep a roomful of young children quiet and attentive while one of their peers struggles to say what she's thinking. Fortunately, Shawn, the classroom teacher, had been working with her students on how to listen to one another during class meetings, and her students were being very patient and respectful. As Rosa explained her strategy, I represented her thinking on the board, making her thoughts visible for the class:

1 + 5 +   1 + 5 =
1   2, 3, 4, 5, 6   7   8, 9, 10, 11, 12

I called on Tim next. "What strategy did you use?" I asked.

"I know my doubles, so five and five is ten and two more is twelve," he explained, with almost no effort whatsoever. I rewrote the number string and recorded Tim's thinking like this:

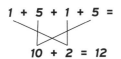

Next, I wrote another number string on the board:

8 + 1 + 3 + 2 =

After giving students time to think about the problem, I asked them to talk to a partner about their strategy. Partner talk allows more students to participate, and it can provide a safe environment in which to share ideas. After a minute or so, I asked the students for their attention and elicited strategies from a few of them.

Toby explained his reasoning: "I just started at eight and kept counting on. Like eight, nine, ten, eleven, twelve; then I counted on two more and it's fourteen."

Below the number string, I represented Toby's thinking like this:

$8 + 1 + 3 + \quad\quad 2 =$
$8 \quad 9 \quad 10, 11, 12 \quad 13, 14$

Next, Danielle said, "I made a ten from the eight and the two. Then I added on four. Ten and four is fourteen."

As I did with Tim's strategy earlier, I used lines to make Danielle's thinking visible:

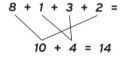

Before finishing this classroom activity, I summarized for the students all of the strategies they had used for solving the number strings. I recorded names for their methods on a chart for later reference:

Counting on
Making tens
Using doubles

Extending the Activity

Different number strings can be used in the classroom as the year progresses. For instance, if the goal is for students to practice finding combinations of ten (e.g., 1 + 9, 8 + 2, 7 + 3, and so on), number strings like these could be useful:

$3 + 2 + 8 = \quad\quad 1 + 4 + 6 + 9 = \quad\quad 4 + 3 + 1 + 7 =$

If the goal is for students to practice finding doubles (e.g., 2 + 2, 3 + 3, 4 + 4, and so on), or near doubles (2 + 3, 3 + 4, 4 + 5, and so on), these number strings would be beneficial:

$4 + 2 + 1 + 4 = \quad\quad 7 + 10 + 7 = \quad\quad 2 + 2 + 5 + 3 =$
$2 + 3 + 6 + 7 = \quad\quad 7 + 8 + 1 + 2 =$

Number strings can be adjusted for various purposes. For example, if students are learning about money and the goal is to learn how to find the total value of a mixed collection of coins, the following number strings could be useful because they include numbers that match coin values (e.g., penny, nickel, dime, quarter, half-dollar):

$$25 + 10 + 5 + 5 = \qquad 1 + 5 + 5 + 10 = \qquad 10 + 50 + 5 + 10 =$$

Number strings provide students valuable practice with combining numbers in efficient ways. Try the following when teaching this class activity:

- Make interlocking cubes available for students to use. The cubes support those children who need to make concrete representations of the problem.

22

People Sorting

For Grades K–2

CONTENT AREA

Algebra

MATERIALS

TIME

five minutes (ten to fifteen minutes to introduce the activity on the first day)

Overview

This activity provides students with opportunities to identify likenesses and differences and to sort students into two groups according to a predetermined rule. Later, children brainstorm rules to sort their classmates into two groups. A new rule is chosen and the activity is repeated.

Activity Directions

1. Think of a rule for sorting students into two different groups, for example, children with shoelaces and children without shoelaces. Don't tell the students your rule.
2. Using your rule, sort volunteers into two groups.
3. Have students guess your rule for sorting.
4. With the students, brainstorm different ways to sort students into two groups.
5. Repeat Steps 1–3, using a new rule for sorting.

Key Questions

- What's my rule for sorting? How do you know?
- What are some different ways we could sort two groups of students?

From the Classroom

"I'm going to sort some of you in two groups and I want you to think about my rule for sorting," Elisabeth Frausto explained. "Everyone sit at the back of the rug and I'll call one student up at a time."

Elisabeth's students were familiar with sorting and classifying lessons and were ready to experience *People Sorting*.

"I'm thinking of how I'll sort you," Elisabeth said. She asked Donavyn to come up and stand to her right.

"Face your classmates, Donavyn," she said.

Elisabeth then asked Justin to stand next to Donavyn and directed Michael and Lizette to stand to her left.

　　　Justin　　　Michael　　　　　　Donavyn　　　Lizette

"Thumbs up when you know my rule," Elisabeth said. After giving her students several seconds of think time, she called on Angie.

"I think your rule is about shoelaces," Angie said.

"How do you know?" Elisabeth asked her.

Angie pointed to Donavyn and Justin and said, "Because those two have shoelaces and the other two don't."

"Does everyone in a group have to have the same attribute?" Elisabeth asked, pointing to Donavyn and Justin. Students nodded in agreement. The word *attribute* was familiar to the students; Elisabeth had used the word in context many times in other sorting activities.

"Let's check," Elisabeth said. "Do Donavyn and Justin have shoelaces?"

"Yes!" the students answered.

"So Donavyn and Justin have the same attribute—they both have shoelaces. And what about Michael and Lizette? They don't have shoelaces, do they?"

After clarifying the rules of the sorting game, Elisabeth acknowledged that Angie's guess was correct. Then she dismissed the four students back to the rug and asked the class a question. "What are some different ways we could sort students into two groups?"

"One group could be girls and the other boys," Tiara suggested.

"How about buttons and no buttons?" Donavyn asked.

"Maybe some kids have long hair and some kids have short hair," Emme added.

"Those are all good ideas," Elisabeth said.

Next, Elisabeth told the students that she was thinking of another rule for sorting. She then directed Gabriella and Areysi to stand to her left and asked Kent to stand on her right.

"Does anyone think they know what my rule for sorting is?" Elisabeth asked.

"I think one group has sweaters and one group doesn't," Tobias guessed.

"Tobias, do you know for sure or do you need more information?" Elisabeth asked.

"I'm pretty sure, but I think I need more information," Tobias responded.

Elisabeth then asked, "Who thinks they know the rule and wants to come and join the group you think you belong in? Serena?"

Serena walked up and joined Kent.

"Serena, why did you join that group?" Elisabeth probed.

"'Cause I don't have a sweater and the people in the other group have sweaters," she explained.

"You're correct," Elisabeth confirmed. "My rule is that one group has sweaters and the other group doesn't have sweaters."

Serena   Kent   Gabriella   Areysi

After dismissing Kent, Gabriella, Serena, and Areysi back to their places on the rug, Elisabeth asked Elianna to stand in front of the class. She then turned to the rest of the students and asked, "Do you know my rule yet?"

The children giggled. "No, there's only one person up there," Emme noted. "You need two groups to see the rule."

"So you need more information?" Elisabeth asked. The students nodded in agreement. Elisabeth then proceeded to call several students up to the front of the rug, sorting them into two groups.

"What's the same about all of these children?" she asked, pointing to the group on her right. "And what's the same about all of these?" she continued, pointing to her left. She gave the students some time to think and then called on Michael and asked him to come and sort himself. Michael joined Kent and Justin. The other group included Angie, Elianna, and Emme.

"You're in the correct group, Michael," Elisabeth said. "Now do you know what my rule is?" she asked the class.

After some giggles, David guessed, "One group is all girls and the other is boys." Everyone seemed to agree and Elisabeth confirmed that his guess was correct.

To finish the activity, Elisabeth called on Nico to think of a rule for sorting and proceeded to help him lead the activity. Asking students to be "the teacher" is motivating for them and gives the teacher a chance to see if students can apply what they've learned.

Extending the Activity

On subsequent days, continue to sort children into two groups and have students guess your rule for sorting. Allow students to lead the guessing game using their own rule for sorting.

Following are some ideas for sorting students into two groups:

- long hair, short hair
- buttons on shirt, no buttons on shirt
- stripes, no stripes
- writing on clothing, no writing on clothing
- wearing sneakers, not wearing sneakers
- long pants, short pants
- sweaters or jackets, no sweaters or jackets
- belts, no belts
- missing front teeth, no missing front teeth
- socks, no socks

23

CONTENT AREA

Data Analysis and Probability

Number and Operations

MATERIALS

TIME

ten minutes

Quick Surveys

For Grades K-2

Overview

Survey questions can be interesting and motivating ways to engage children in collecting, organizing, and interpreting data. These questions should be taken from the interests of the children and experiences that occur in their daily lives.

In this activity, students learn how data can be organized using different types of graphs. Interpreting data on a graph provides students with valuable practice in counting, addition, subtraction, and using the concepts of greater than, less than, and equal. In the lesson for second grade, students are exposed to one type of statistical average: the mode (the number or numbers that appear in a set of data most often).

There are several different types of graphs. Real graphs use actual objects (e.g., students, shoes). Picture graphs use pictures or models to stand for real things. And symbolic graphs are the most abstract and use symbols such as tally marks or Xs. In the primary grades, data on symbolic graphs are most typically displayed using Venn diagrams, line plots, bar graphs, and circle graphs. Whichever type of graph is used, it is important that students have experiences that focus on discussing and interpreting the data collected.

Activity Directions for Grades K-1

1. Draw a graph on the board that does not include a question. For example:

Shoelaces | **No Shoelaces**

2. Ask students what they think the survey question will be.
3. Collect data from some of the students.
4. Ask the students what they can say about the graph so far.
5. Collect more data from the students.
6. Elicit statements about the data from students, and record their words on the board. Ask the class where the math words are in the statements made about the data. Highlight the math words in the sentences.

Key Questions

- What do you think my survey question will be?
- What can we say about the graph so far?
- What sentence can we write about the data on the graph?
- Where are the math words in _____'s sentence?

Activity Directions for Grade 2

1. Pose a question to students that could be answered by conducting a survey, or have students generate a question.
2. Collect data from students and create a graph based on the data gathered.
3. Process the graph with students by asking them questions (see "Key Questions" section, below).

Key Questions

- What do you think my survey question will be?
- What do you notice about the graph?
- What can we say about the graph so far?
- Which has the most number of Xs (responses)? Which is most popular?
- Which has the least number of Xs (responses)?
- How many more Xs does _____ have than _____?

From a Kindergarten and First-Grade Classroom

Elisabeth Frausto's students were huddled on the classroom rug. Elisabeth had drawn a graph on the board that looked like this:

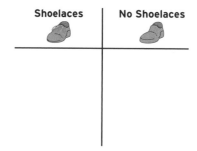

After reading aloud the chart to the class, Elisabeth said, "Turn to the person next to you and tell what you think the survey question will be." Elisabeth likes to start with an open-ended question because it challenges students' thinking. After about fifteen seconds, Elisabeth called on a volunteer.

"It will be about shoelaces and no shoelaces," Katie guessed.

"What question do you think I'll ask?" Elisabeth probed.

"If you have shoelaces put an X in one spot, and if you don't have shoelaces put an X in the other spot," Ray said.

Elisabeth sensed that students were having trouble generating a question, so she helped by providing a prompt.

"Let's think of a question I'll ask," Elisabeth began. "Think about shoelaces. Do you . . ."

"Do you have shoelaces!" several students exclaimed.

Elisabeth acknowledged the students' response and then wrote the question *Do you have shoelaces?* above the graph on the board. The students read the words as Elisabeth read them aloud.

Next, Elisabeth told the students to check whether they had shoelaces or not. She then recorded data on the class graph:

Do you have Shoelaces?

Shoelaces	No Shoelaces
X X X	X X
X X X	X X

"What can we say about the graph now?" Elisabeth asked.

"*Shoelaces* has more!" Sophie exclaimed. "I know by just looking at it."

"*No Shoelaces* has four," Justin said.

"How do you know?" Elisabeth asked.

"'Cause two and two is four," he responded.

Elisabeth then collected and recorded more data from the students. When the entire class had responded, the graph looked like this:

Do you have Shoelaces?

Shoelaces	No Shoelaces
X X X	X X
X X X	X X
X X X	X X
	X X

"How can we find out how many students have shoelaces?" Elisabeth asked the class.

"Count!" several students exclaimed.

As Elisabeth touched each X, the class counted the total number of Xs on each side of the graph. Elisabeth recorded the numbers:

Do you have Shoelaces?

Shoelaces	No Shoelaces
X X X	X X
X X X	X X
X X X	X X
	X X
9	8

"What sentence can we write about the data on the graph?" Elisabeth said. She waited several seconds before calling on Tobias.

"*Shoelaces* is more," he stated.

"So you mean more students have shoelaces?" Elisabeth asked, rephrasing Tobias's sentence.

Once he nodded his agreement, Elisabeth wrote Tobias's sentence on the board next to the graph:

More students have shoelaces.

"Where are the math words in Tobias's sentence?"

"*More*!" Serena offered excitedly. "*More* is a math word."

Elisabeth then drew a box around the word *more*:

$\boxed{More}$ *students have shoelaces.*

What's another sentence we can write about the data on the graph?" Elisabeth asked.

"*No Shoelaces* has less," Jamal offered.

Elisabeth wrote Jamal's sentence on the board like this:

"No shoelaces" has less.

"Where are the math words in Jamal's sentence?" Elisabeth asked the class.

"The math word is *less*," Sophie said. "*Less* is also on our math word chart."

Elisabeth acknowledged Sophie's observation and then drew a box around the word *less* on the board:

"No shoelaces" has $\boxed{less}$.

"Let's think of a sentence that has a number in it," Elisabeth prompted.

"There are nine people who have shoelaces and eight people who don't," David said. "*Eight* and *nine* are the math words in my sentence."

Elisabeth wrote David's sentence and drew boxes around the math words:

There are $\boxed{nine}$ people who have shoelaces and $\boxed{eight}$ people who don't.

Elisabeth finished the activity by having the students read aloud the three sentences that described the data on the graph.

From a Second-Grade Classroom

Shawn Yoshimoto's second graders came in from recess and settled on the rug in the front of the classroom. I had drawn a graph on the board in order to collect some data from the students. I wanted to survey the children to find out which restaurant they preferred.

There are many questions one could use to survey young children for this activity (see suggestions for quick survey questions on pages 126 and 127). Better yet, students can come up with their own questions. The graph that I used with Shawn's class looked like this:

Which restaurant is your favorite?

McDonald's	Burger King	Wendy's	Jack in the Box

After we read aloud the question and the choices together, I asked the students to each think about which restaurant was their favorite and then raise their hand when they'd made a decision. To expedite the process, I elicited preferences from the students and recorded Xs on the graph myself rather than have each child come up and individually respond. Here's what the graph looked like when it was complete:

Which restaurant is your favorite?

McDonald's	Burger King	Wendy's	Jack in the Box
X X X		X X X X X	X X X X X
		X X X X	X X X X X X

"What do you notice about our graph?" I asked the class.

"Nobody picked Burger King," Yesenia said.

"Not very many people like McDonald's," Alexis observed.

The room grew quiet. I waited and then asked the question again. "What else do you notice?"

There was no response. "Which restaurant is most popular in our room? Which has the most Xs?" I asked.

"Jack in the Box!" students chorused.

"Are you sure? Who can prove it?" I challenged.

Shirin volunteered. "I counted the Xs for Jack in the Box and there's eleven. Then I counted the Xs for Wendy's and there's nine, and eleven is two more than nine."

"So Jack in the Box has the most Xs," I summarized. "Mathematicians would say that Jack in the Box is the mode. The mode in this case is the name of the restaurant that was chosen the most."

"Make sense?" I asked the class after giving them a moment to think. Students nodded in agreement.

"If Jack in the Box has the most, which restaurant is the least popular? Which restaurant has the least number of Xs?" I asked.

"Burger King has the least; it doesn't have any," Yesenia said. "That's what I was talking about before. Nobody picked Burger King."

"What else do you notice?" I asked the class.

"Wendy's has more than McDonald's," Demonte said.

Here was an opportunity to pose a problem that involved comparing two quantities. Even if Demonte hadn't made his observation, I was prepared to ask the following question. "How many more people like Wendy's than McDonald's?" I waited several seconds, giving students time to figure. Then I began calling on volunteers.

"I looked at the three Xs for McDonald's," Tony began. "Then I took off three Xs for Wendy's and then I counted the rest of the Xs on Wendy's and it's six. So Wendy's has six more than McDonald's."

Osman explained, "Wendy's has nine and McDonald's has three, and nine minus three is six."

"I used counting up," Xitlalic said. "I started with McDonald's and that's three. And I counted on my fingers until I got to nine. I used six fingers."

"I know that three plus six is nine," Demonte added.

From conversations like this, students learn that there are many different strategies for solving problems. Also, graphs provide an ideal context for talking about numbers and operations.

Extending the Activity

There are many questions that can be used to survey students. Following are examples of survey questions that ask for both factual information and students' opinions:

- What's your favorite TV show?
- How many pencils are there in your desk?
- How many letters are in your first name?
- What's your favorite ice-cream flavor?
- Do you have a younger brother or sister?
- Do you have a middle name?

- Are you wearing shoes that have laces or no laces?
- Is your hair straight or curly?
- Will you buy your lunch today?
- Are you left-handed or right-handed?
- What color are your eyes?
- Do you think children should earn an allowance?
- Which subject in school is your favorite?
- Which pets do you have at home?

24

Race to 20

For Grades K–2

CONTENT AREA

Number and Operations

MATERIALS

- chart paper
- markers or chalk in a variety of colors
- die with faces labeled 1–6

TIME

ten minutes (fifteen minutes to introduce the activity on the first day)

Overview

In this math activity, the teacher plays a game against the class to see who can reach the target number of 20 first. The teams (the teacher and the class) take turns rolling a die to see how many boxes to color in on a game board.

Race to 20 provides children with experience relating a given number to other numbers, specifically to 10 and 20. For example, 14 is 10 and 4 more; 8 is 2 less than 10; and 15 is 5 less than 20. The game can also help children see that ten individual objects become one group of ten, an important idea that underlies the understanding of place value.

Race to 20 also involves students in comparing quantities (Who has more? How many more?), visualizing numbers, seeing part-whole relationships ($20 = 3 + 5 + 6 + 1 + 5$), and connecting quantities to number combinations (we need 2 more to make 10 because $8 + 2 = 10$). In addition, the game can help students think about equivalence. For example, students learn that 10 is equivalent to $8 + 2$ and $5 + 5$ and $9 + 1$ and so on.

Activity Directions

1. Draw a game board on the chart paper.

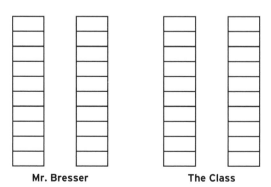

Mr. Bresser   The Class

2. Teams (the teacher and the class) take turns rolling a 1–6 die. After each roll, a player colors in the number of boxes (using a different color on each roll) that corresponds with the number shown on the die. Play continues until one team reaches or goes over 20 (a team does not have to reach 20 exactly).

Key Questions

- Who's ahead? By how much? How do you know?
- How many more to make ten? How do you know?
- How many more to make twenty? How do you know?
- How many tens are there in twenty? How do you know?

From the Classroom

After Frannie MacKenzie's students had finished completing some of their other classroom activities, such as singing songs and reading the classroom rules together, I introduced *Race to 20*. On the whiteboard, I drew a game board like this:

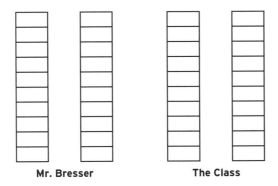

Mr. Bresser   The Class

"Today we're going to play a game using this game board," I told the class, pointing to the four columns, or towers, with ten boxes in each.

I told the students that two of the towers were mine, and the other two towers were theirs. After the students determined that there were twenty boxes (ten in each tower) for each team, I explained how to play *Race to 20*.

"We're going to take turns rolling the die," I began. "When it's my turn, I'll roll the die. The number that comes up on the die will tell me how many boxes in one of my towers to color in. Then I'll choose a volunteer to play for the class."

I started the game by rolling a 6 on the die and using a red marker to color in each of the first six boxes in one of my towers. I then called on Maureen to play for the class. She rolled a 3 and colored in each of the first three boxes in one of the class's towers. The game board now looked like this:

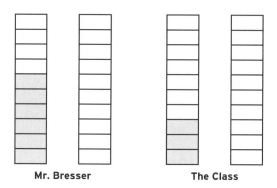

"Who's ahead?" I asked.

"You are!" students responded.

"How many more do I have?" This seemed to be a difficult question for these K–1 students, so I decided to reword it.

"Which is more? Six or three?" I asked, pointing to my six boxes and their three boxes respectively.

"Six!"

"How many more do you need to get to six?" This time a few students raised their hands.

"Three more, 'cause three and three makes six," Sarah said.

Next it was my turn. I rolled a 1 and used a blue marker to color in one box above the six red ones in my tower. Tyron volunteered for the class. He rolled a 5 and used a blue marker to color in five boxes in the class's tower. Now the game board looked like this:

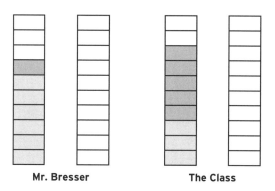

"We're winning!" several students exclaimed.

"We're ahead by one!" someone shouted. The students were really excited now. Although I had to ask them several times to sit "crisscross" and raise their hands to speak, I was pleased that all of the comments I heard were math related.

"How many more do I need to make ten?" I asked.

"Three," Jill answered. "Can't you see the three empty boxes?"

"We only need two more," Tyron noticed. "That's because eight and two make ten." Tyron consistently made connections between the quantities represented and number combinations.

On our next set of turns, I rolled another 1 and a student volunteer rolled a 6. This really got everyone excited. Our game board now looked like this:

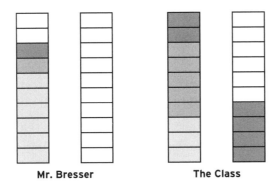

Mr. Bresser   The Class

"How many does the class have now?" I asked.

"We have fourteen 'cause ten plus four is fourteen," Cody said. Cody didn't have to count the first ten boxes; he just knew there were ten, and then he counted on from there.

"Hey, I know something!" Betina exclaimed. "If you have fourteen, the one is the ten boxes," she said, pointing to the class's tower that was completely colored in, "and the four boxes on the other side is the four, and that makes fourteen."

Betina was on to something. She seemed to understand the value of the digits in the number 14, an important idea in understanding place value.

I wrote the number *14* under the class's towers; I then pointed to the 1 in 14 and the tower that had ten boxes colored in, as Betina had done. Next I pointed to the tower with four boxes colored in and the 4 in 14.

"Is that what you mean?" I asked. Betina nodded her head in agreement.

"How many more does the class need to make twenty?" I asked. My question was met with silence. I waited for a few seconds until a couple of hands went up; then I called on Ramon.

"We need six more," he offered. "I just counted the empty boxes."

"Let's count to check if Ramon is correct," I said. Together we counted as I touched each of the six remaining boxes.

When we were finished with *Race to 20*, the game board represented the quantities obtained by rolling the die in two ways: visually, with the colored-in boxes, and symbolically, with numbers. The students could easily see all the parts that made up the total scores of 15 and 20.

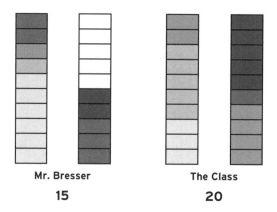

To help the students make the connection between my score of 15 and the different rolls that made up 15, I recorded my score like this underneath the game board:

15 = 6 + 1 + 1 + 5 + 2

As I read each number in the equation, I pointed to the corresponding colored-in boxes on the game board to show the quantity that the number represented. I did the same for the class's score:

20 = 3 + 5 + 6 + 1 + 5

Extending the Activity

Race to 20 can be played with the whole class or with a small group of students, or partners could play the game during math time.

Sampling Tiles

For Grades K-2

25

Overview

In the primary grades, students are expected to develop and evaluate inferences and make predictions that are based on data. In this activity, students make predictions about the contents of a paper bag based on a sample of data.

Activity Directions

1. Using two different colors, place a combination of ten tiles or cubes inside a paper bag.
2. Show the students the bag and tell them how many tiles or cubes are in the bag.
3. Ask a volunteer to come to the board and use tally marks to keep a record of the number of times a certain color is pulled from the bag.
4. Model how to pull one tile or cube out of the bag and replace it without peeking inside.
5. Continue having students sample and replace tiles or cubes until you have gathered ten pieces of data. Then ask the students to predict whether there are more tiles of one color than the other, or whether they think there is an equal number of each color inside the bag.
6. Collect another ten pieces of data. If there are more than twenty students in the class, collect an additional ten pieces of data to ensure that everyone gets a chance to sample. Ask students to predict again.
7. Take the tiles or cubes out of the bag and count them.

Key Questions

- What color might be pulled from the bag? Explain.
- Do think there are more yellow tiles or red tiles inside the bag? Explain.
- Do you think there is an equal number of yellow and red tiles inside the bag? Explain.

CONTENT AREA

Data Analysis and Probability

Number and Operations

MATERIALS

- small paper bag
- total of 10 color tiles or cubes in two different colors

TIME

ten minutes

- How many times have we pulled a red tile from the bag? How many times have we pulled a yellow tile from the bag? Explain how you figured it out.
- If there were ___ red tiles in the bag, how many yellow tiles would there be? Explain.

From the Classroom

I held up a small paper bag for Elisabeth Frausto's students to see. Inside there were three yellow tiles and seven red tiles, hidden from view. "I have some little square tiles in this bag. Some are red and some are yellow," I began.

"How many are in there?" Donavyn asked.

"Well, I have ten tiles altogether," I answered. "Your job is to figure out whether there are more red tiles, more yellow tiles, or whether there is an equal, or same, number of red and yellow tiles."

"Show us!" several students exclaimed.

"No, I'm not going to show you," I said. The class responded with a collective groan.

"I'm not going to show you yet," I told the students. "First, we're going to collect some data, or information, to help us figure out whether there are more yellow tiles or more red tiles, or if there is the same number of each. I need a volunteer to record tally marks on the board."

The students were eager to offer their help. I called on Sophie, who came up to the board. I wrote the words *Red* and *Yellow* on the board:

Red
Yellow

I then demonstrated what the students were to do. Without looking, I reached inside the bag with my hand and pulled out a tile. It was red. I directed Sophie to put a tally mark next to the word *Red* on the board:

Red |
Yellow

I then placed the tile back in the bag and shook it. Before asking Saul to pull a tile from the bag, I asked the class a question.

"Saul is going to pull the next tile out of the bag," I said. "What color might he pull out?" This seemed like an obvious question, but I wanted students to think about the idea that only two things could happen: Saul could pull either a red tile or a yellow tile.

"Red!" several students exclaimed.

"Or yellow!" others chimed in.

"Are you sure? Who can explain why there could be only yellow or red?" I asked.

"You said there were only red and yellow tiles in the bag," Roger reminded us.

"That's right, Roger," I confirmed. "When we reach into the bag, only two things can happen: we can pull out a red tile or a yellow tile."

Saul reached into the bag. I reminded him not to peek as he pulled out a tile. He removed a red tile. I directed Sophie to record another tally mark by the word *Red*. We continued in this fashion until we had collected ten pieces of data. The class chart then looked like this:

Red |JHt| |||
Yellow ||

The students enjoyed this activity and cheered after each tile was pulled. Most were rooting for red, but a few were holding out for yellow to come up the most. What was important, however, was that the students were actively engaged in collecting data and making predictions. After we had collected the first ten pieces of data, I asked the class a question.

"I want you to think about what's inside the bag," I began. "Think about whether there are more yellow tiles, more red tiles, or about the same, or equal, number of yellows and reds inside."

After giving the students a few seconds to think, I said, "Raise your hand if you think there are more yellow tiles inside the bag." Only two students raised their hands.

"What about red tiles? Who thinks there are more red ones inside the bag?" This time, most of the students raised their hands.

"Does anyone think there is an equal, or same, number of yellow and red tiles in the bag?" No one raised a hand.

"Who can explain why you think there are more red or yellow tiles inside the bag?" I asked. A few students raised their hands, and after pausing to wait for more hands, I called on Serena.

"I think most of the tiles in the bag are red," Serena predicted.

"What do you mean by *most*?" I asked her. "About how many red tiles do you think are in the bag?"

"Almost ten, like nine maybe," she responded.

"If there were nine red tiles, how many yellow ones would there be?" I asked. "Talk to a partner about what you think." I waited several seconds to allow for partner talk, and then I called on Angie.

"If there was nine red ones, then there would be one yellow, 'cause nine and one make ten," she explained.

"Other ideas?" I asked. There were no hands raised, so we continued to gather ten more pieces of data. When we were through, the class chart looked like this:

Red ||||| ||||| |||
Yellow ||||| ||

"Now we have more information to help our predictions," I said. "How many times have we pulled a red tile and how many times have we pulled a yellow tile?"

I gave the students several seconds to count the tally marks, and then I asked for someone to share his answer and explain his thinking. I called on Zuriel.

"We pulled out a red tile thirteen times," he reported.

"How did you count the tallies, Zuriel?" I probed.

"I counted by ones, and I got thirteen red and seven yellow."

"Did anyone count in a different way?" I asked.

"I counted by fives and I got the same as Zuriel," Katie said.

As a class, we counted the tally marks by ones and then by fives to check. Then I asked the students another question.

"Raise your hand if you think there are more red tiles in the bag." Most of the students raised their hands. When I asked if anyone thought there were more yellow tiles, there were still a few holdouts.

Gathering another set of ten tiles would have given us a larger sample size and more information from which to make predictions. However, I decided to finish up the activity, and I spilled the tiles onto the rug. Even without counting, the students could see that there were more red tiles. To make sure, we counted the tiles together as I touched each tile to model one-to-one correspondence.

Extending the Activity

- To help students think about the addends that make 10, ask them what are the possible combinations of tiles that could be inside the bag (e.g., 9 red, 1 yellow; 8 red, 2 yellow; 7 red, 3 yellow; and so forth) and record the combinations on the board. Then ask students which tile combination they think is inside the bag.

- Before revealing what is inside the bag, collect larger sample sizes of data. For example, when this experiment is done with forty or fifty draws from the bag, the initial predictions based on the first ten draws will change as you gather additional data. Typically, students' predictions about what is inside the bag will improve if they have a larger sample size from which to make their predictions.

Ten-Frames

For Grades K–2

CONTENT AREA

Number and
Operations

MATERIALS

TIME

ten minutes

Overview

In this classroom activity, students determine the total number of dots inside a ten-frame. A ten-frame is simply a 2-by-5 array in which counters or dots are placed to illustrate numbers. In this classroom activity, ten-frames are used to help children visualize and count quantities in different ways.

Activity Directions

1. Draw a ten-frame on the board:

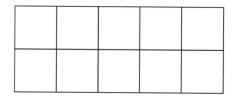

2. Ask students to determine the total number of boxes in the frame. Discuss.
3. Draw a number of dots inside the ten-frame, placing only one dot in each box. Ask students to determine the total number of dots, calling on several different volunteers to explain their thinking.

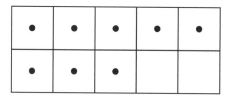

4. Repeat Step 3, changing the number of dots inside the ten-frame.

Key Questions

- How many boxes are in the ten-frame? How did you figure it out?
- How else could we figure out whether there are ten boxes in the ten-frame?
- How many dots are inside the ten-frame? How did you figure it out? Who has another way to figure it out?

From the Classroom

After spending a few minutes having Frannie MacKenzie's students count dot arrangements (see "Dots" on page 47), I introduced a new classroom activity called *Ten-Frames*. First I drew a picture of a ten-frame on the board:

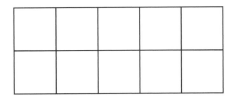

"This sort of looks like a window frame," I began, pointing to my drawing and then to the windows on one side of the classroom. "How many boxes are in the frame if this is one box?" I asked, pointing to one of the boxes in the ten-frame. After a few seconds, lots of children raised their hands.

"Let's all say the answer together in a whisper voice," I directed.

Most students said "Ten!" Some students responded with "Nine," and a few others said there were eight boxes. I think that it was difficult for some students to count the boxes from afar.

"Who would like to show and tell how you figured out the answer?" I asked. I called on Renee.

"There's ten boxes," she said.

"Can you come up and show us how you counted?" I asked. Renee came up to the board and counted the boxes one by one as the other students counted with her. This was good counting practice for the students, helping them see that one number name stands for one object that is counted. It is crucial for students to understand one-to-one correspondence in order to count correctly.

"How else could we count to make sure there are ten boxes?" I asked the class.

"By twos!" Carlos offered.

"Let's try," I said. We counted the boxes together by twos as I touched pairs of boxes. Then we counted by fives, as suggested by another child.

"The frame is called a *ten-frame* because there are ten boxes inside," I told the class. "OK, now I'm going to draw some dots inside the ten-frame, with just one dot in each box."

I proceeded to draw three dots in the ten-frame:

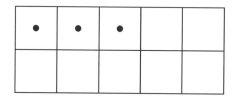

When I asked how many dots there were, everyone seemed to know that there were three dots immediately without having to count them. Some students explained that they knew there were three because it was "two less than five." Only one student reported that he counted the dots one by one.

Next I drew eight dots in the ten-frame:

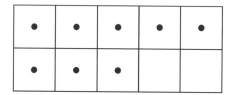

"How many dots are there?" I asked.

"Eight," Jarrod said. "I see five; then I counted three more."

"So you saw five, and then what?" I asked, probing a little to find out whether Jarrod had used his knowledge of addition facts (5 + 3) or counted on from five. I asked him to come up to the board and show us.

"I did five," he said, pointing to the five dots on the top of the frame, "then I did six, seven, eight."

Having students like Jarrod model their thinking helps other students see that strategies like counting on are viable. If no one had used the strategy of counting on, I might have modeled it for students.

"How about another way to figure the number of dots?" I asked.

"I counted by ones," Monica said.

I asked Monica to come up to the board and show us, and as she pointed to each dot, the class counted aloud with her.

"Any other ways?" I asked.

"I know that there's ten in all, and I know that eight plus two more is ten," explained Carlos.

The students' strategies represented a range of mathematical thinking, from counting from one, to counting on, to making use of addition. Keeping track of which strategies students use to solve problems is important. And helping them acquire new, more sophisticated strategies (like Carlos's) is an important goal.

For the next five minutes or so, I continued to change the number of dots inside the ten-frame by erasing some and adding some more. Each time, I asked the students to determine the number of dots and asked them how they figured it out.

Extending the Activity

After students gain experience working with one ten-frame, have them count the dots inside two ten-frames positioned one above the other, like this:

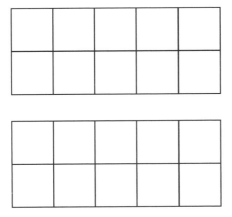

Using two ten-frames extends students' work with numbers beyond ten. It also helps students think about groupings of ten, an important idea for developing the concept of place value.

27

Ten-Frames Cleared

For Grades K–2

CONTENT AREA

Number and
Operations
Data Analysis and
Probability

MATERIALS

- ten-frames, 1 each
  for grades K-1
  students; 2 each
  for grade 2
  students (see
  Blackline Masters)
- interlocking cubes,
  10 each for grades
  K-1 students; 20
  each for grade 2
  students
- die numbered 0-5
  (or substitute the
  numerals with dot
  arrangements) for
  grades K-1
  students; die
  numbered 1-6 for
  grade 2 students

TIME

ten minutes (fifteen
to twenty minutes to
introduce the activity
on the first day)

Overview

Ten-frames are 2-by-5 arrays in which counters or dots are placed to illustrate numbers. In this math activity, students begin by filling ten-frames with cubes, placing one cube in each box. The teacher (or a student volunteer) rolls a die. The students then remove that number of cubes from their ten-frames. Play continues until the ten-frames are cleared of cubes. *Ten-Frames Cleared* provides children practice with subtracting one quantity from another. The activity can also be used to introduce probability.

Activity Directions

1. Distribute materials for the activity and discuss them with the students.
2. Have students fill their ten-frames with cubes, placing one cube in each box.
3. Each time you or a student volunteer rolls the die, have students remove that number of cubes from their ten-frames.
4. Continue to roll until students' ten-frames are cleared. Use tally marks on the board to keep track of the number of rolls it takes to empty the ten-frames.

Key Questions

- Why is the frame called a ten-frame? Explain.
- How many cubes are left on your ten-frame? How do you know?
- How many rolls do you think it will take to clear the ten-frame? Explain.
- How many more rolls do you think it will take to clear the ten-frame? Explain.
- What is the least number of rolls it will take to clear the ten-frame? Explain. (Answer: If you use a 0–5 die, the least number of rolls

would be two if you rolled a 5 each time.) If you use a 1–6 die, the least number of rolls would still be two. If students used two ten-frames, it would take four rolls to clear the frame using a 0–5 die and four rolls using a 1–6 die.

From a Kindergarten and First-Grade Classroom

I distributed one ten-frame and ten Snap Cubes to each of the twenty students in Frannie MacKenzie's class. The students were seated on the carpet in the front of the room, ready to learn about a new math activity. Frannie's students were familiar with the ten-frames, having played the game *Grow and Shrink* (see page 76) several times during the past week.

"Today we're going to use a different die," I began. "Rather than use a die that has dots on it, we're going to use one that has numbers on it to play a new game called *Ten-Frames Cleared*." I showed the students the number on each face of the new die. I then drew a picture of a ten-frame on the board:

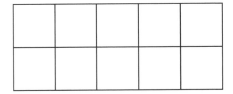

"Why do you think the frame is called a ten-frame?" I asked.

"Because it has ten boxes inside," Sarah said.

"How do you know?" I asked her.

"Because five and five is ten," she responded. Together with the class, I counted the boxes, first by fives and then by ones, to check Sarah's idea.

"To play *Ten-Frames Cleared*," I continued, "you have to start with ten cubes in your frame, one in each box." I then directed the students to each fill their ten-frame with ten Snap Cubes. This was easy for them since they'd had plenty of prior experience with the frames.

I then began giving directions for the game. "OK, now we're ready to play. I'm going to roll the die. The number that comes up on the die will tell us how many cubes we have to take off of our ten-frames. We're going to see how many rolls it will take to clear our ten-frames. I'm going to keep track of how many rolls by making tally marks on the board. Ready?"

It took three rolls to clear the ten-frame on the first game. I rolled a 2 on the first roll, a 4 on the second roll, and a 5 on the third roll. Although students had four cubes remaining on their ten-frames when I rolled the 5, I explained that as long as I rolled at least a 4, we could clear the frame. We didn't need to roll exactly 4 to clear the frame. By the end of the first game, I had recorded three tally marks on the board, representing the three rolls it took to clear the ten-frame.

As I rolled and tallied during the game, I observed the children at work. In Frannie's class there was a wide range of abilities, typical of many classrooms. When students had to take away cubes from their ten-frames and count how many cubes remained, some did so with ease, immediately calling out the number remaining. Others struggled. I noticed one boy just sitting there, not removing any cubes. I reminded him to take off two cubes after the first roll, modeling it for him. We then counted the remaining cubes together. I kept an eye on him and five other students who seemed to have difficulty with the task. After playing a couple of games, all six were able to remove cubes and count what was remaining independently.

At the start of our third and final game, I asked the students to guess how many rolls it would take to clear the ten-frame. I reminded them that for our first game, it took three rolls, and for our second game, it took four rolls.

"I think three rolls!" Carlos guessed.

"Why do you think that?" I asked.

"'Cause the numbers on the dice are not that big," he responded.

"I think five rolls," Alicia offered.

"Why do you think five?" I asked. Alicia shrugged her shoulders.

"Maybe zero rolls!" John exclaimed.

I decided not to push John for an explanation. I realized that thinking about the probability in this game was too difficult for most of these K–1 students. In contrast, I found it easier to ask questions related to probability when I played *Ten-Frames Cleared* with second graders.

From a Second-Grade Classroom

With second graders, I started by giving each student twenty Snap Cubes and two ten-frames, directing them to put the frames on the carpet in front of them like this:

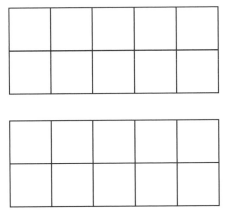

Next I directed the students to put one cube in each of the twenty boxes in their ten-frames. Then I explained that they would be removing the number of cubes that matched the number that came up on the 1–6 die.

"Before we begin playing, I have a question I want you to think about," I said. "How many rolls do you think it will take to empty the ten-frames?"

"What do you mean?" River asked. River wasn't the only student who seemed puzzled by my question.

"Well, could we completely empty the ten-frames in one roll?" I asked.

"No!" several students responded.

"If you rolled a six, you'd still have lots of cubes," Tamika noted.

"What about two rolls?" I probed. "Talk with someone next to you and make a guess. About how many rolls do you think it would take to empty the ten-frames?" After several seconds, I asked my question again and called on Tony.

"I think about five or six rolls," he said. "'Cause if you roll the die, it won't always come up a six. If you rolled a six every time, you could clear the ten-frame in . . . " He hesitated.

"What do you think?" I asked. "If you rolled two sixes in a row, how many cubes is that?"

"Twelve," Tony answered.

"What about if you rolled three sixes in a row?" I continued. "Let's all think about it." After a few seconds I elicited ideas from the students.

"That would be eighteen, 'cause six plus six is twelve, and if you count on six more you get eighteen," Cindy explained.

"So could we clear the ten-frames in three rolls?"

"No, it would take four rolls," Jose replied.

"I think it will take more than four, maybe five or six," River predicted.

"Maybe more, like between five and ten," Miguel added.

After listening to several more guesses from students, we played the game. I asked for a student volunteer to keep track of the number of rolls it took for us to clear the ten-frames by making tally marks on the board. At the end of the game, it had taken us seven rolls to empty the ten-frames. On our final roll, students had two cubes left in one of their frames and I rolled a 5. At first there was some confusion because students thought I needed to roll a 2 to clear the frame. I explained that we just had to clear the frame of cubes on the last roll.

Before playing another game, I again elicited predictions from the students, asking them how many rolls it would take to empty the ten-frames. This time, students began to use the data (the tallies that represented rolls) we had gathered from our first game to inform their predictions. Playing the game more than once and over an extended period of time gave these second graders ongoing practice with both subtraction and probability.

Extending the Activity

Play *Ten-Frames Cleared* over several days and keep track of the number of rolls it takes to clear the ten-frames. Notice if students use these data to help them make predictions.

Dot Arrangements
Fit the Facts Family Letter
Ten-Frames

Dot Arrangements

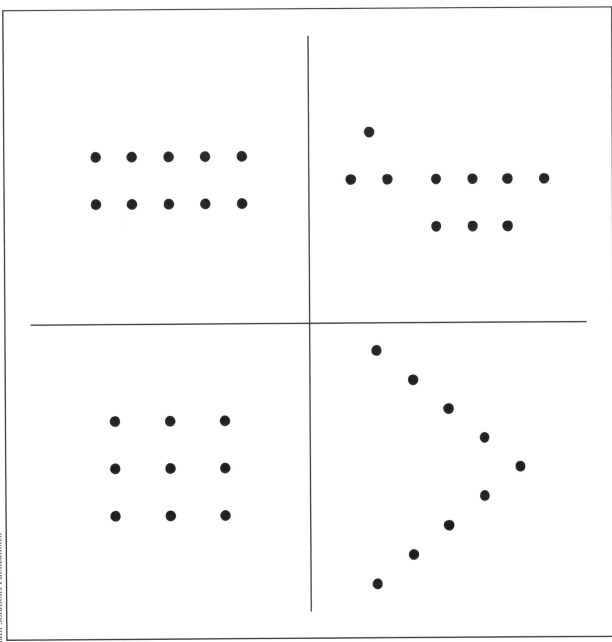

Dot Arrangements

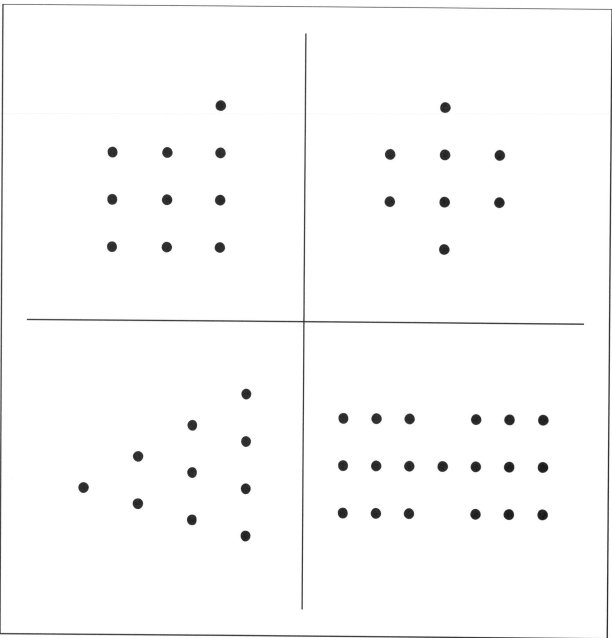

From *Minilessons for Math Practice, Grades K–2* by Rusty Bresser and Caren Holtzman. © 2006 Math Solutions Publications.

Dot Arrangements

From *Minilessons for Math Practice, Grades K–2* by Rusty Bresser and Caren Holtzman. © 2006 Math Solutions Publications.

Fit the Facts Family Letter

Dear Family,

We are doing a math activity at school called *Fit the Facts*, in which the students are learning about how numbers are used in the world. We need your help! Please work with your child and complete the following statements; then return this sheet to school tomorrow. Thanks!

I am _____ years old.
I am in _____ grade.
I live at _____ _____ (street, drive, circle).
I am _____ inches tall.
I live about _____ miles from school.
My favorite number is _____.
I have _____ brothers and _____ sisters.
I have _____ pets.

From *Minilessons for Math Practice, Grades K–2* by Rusty Bresser and Caren Holtzman. © 2006 Math Solutions Publications.

Ten-Frames

From *Minilessons for Math Practice, Grades K–2* by Rusty Bresser and Caren Holtzman. © 2006 Math Solutions Publications.

References

Burns, M. 1994. *The Greedy Triangle*. Illus. Gordon Silveria. New York: Scholastic.

Carpenter, T. P., E. Fennema, M. L. Franke, L. Levi, and S. B. Empson. 1999. *Children's Mathematics: Cognitively Guided Instruction*. Portsmouth, NH: Heinemann.

National Council of Teachers of Mathematics. 2000. *Principles and Standards for School Mathematics*. Reston, VA: NCTM.

Sturges, P. 1995. *Ten Flashing Fireflies*. Illus. Anna Vojtech. New York: North-South.